T0268064

— The Original —

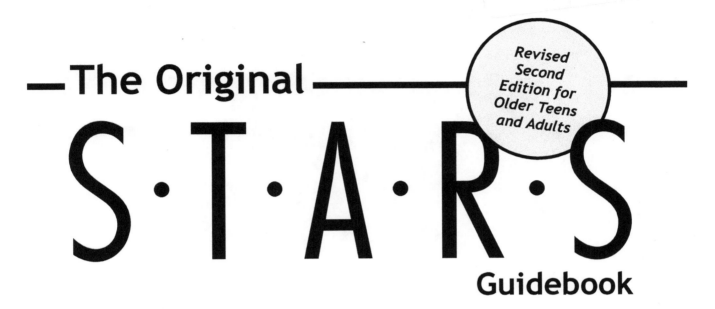

Revised Second Edition for Older Teens and Adults

S·T·A·R·S

Guidebook

Social Skills **T**raining Guide for Teaching **A**ssertiveness, **R**elationship Skills & **S**exual Awareness

Susan Heighway, MS, PNP-BC, APNP & Susan Kidd Webster, MSSW, ISW

The Original S·T·A·R·S Guidebook: Social Skills Training Guide for Teaching Assertiveness, Relationship Skills & Sexual Awareness

All marketing and publishing rights guaranteed to and reserved by:

FUTURE HORIZONS INC.

817-277-0727

817-277-2270 (fax)

E-mail: *info@fhautism.com*

www.fhautism.com

ISBN: 9781949177893

ACKNOWLEDGMENTS

Many colleagues and friends were involved in the completion of this guidebook. It is with deep gratitude that we extend our appreciation and thanks to:

- The Waisman Center, University of Wisconsin-Madison and the Wisconsin Disabilities Board.

- Pat Patterson, who generously shared her expertise, inspiration, and energy with us.

- Cathy Berger, Marsha Shaw, Patricia Mitchell, Yvonne Slusser, Leah Thompson, and Betsy True.

- Marcus Bachhuber, MD for reviewing and updating the Sexual Awareness and Glossary sections.

- Future Horizons, Inc., for their support in editing and publishing the STARS guidebooks.

- The participants with disabilities, their families, and support providers who shared their experiences and stories; we have learned so much from you.

THE AUTHORS

Susan Heighway, MS, PNP-BC, APNP, is emeritus clinical professor with the University Center for Excellence in Disabilities, Waisman Center and School of Nursing, University of Wisconsin-Madison. At the Waisman Center, she worked as a nurse practitioner in the outpatient specialty clinics serving individuals from birth to adulthood with developmental disabilities, genetic or metabolic disorders, and their families. She was also the nursing training coordinator for a federally funded maternal and child health interdisciplinary training program for graduate students.

Susan Kidd Webster, MSSW, ISW, is emeritus faculty of the School of Social Work at the University of Wisconsin-Madison. For many years, she worked on capacity-building projects as an outreach specialist with the Waisman Center to support people with developmental disabilities in the community. She taught courses and coordinated internships for undergraduate and graduate social work students working with persons with developmental disabilities.

Ms. Heighway and Ms. Webster worked together at the Waisman Center and have several years of experience in the area of sexual abuse prevention and sexuality education for people with developmental disabilities. They both served on a task force that was convened by the Wisconsin Council on Developmental Disabilities and addressed issues of sexual abuse for people with developmental disabilities. They provided consultation to community agencies, presented at conferences, gave guest lectures on campus, and conducted workshops regarding sexuality and sexual abuse at the local, state, and national levels. They are the co-authors of *STARS 2*, an adapted version of this guidebook for school-aged children, published by Future Horizons, Inc.

CONTENTS

CONTENTS

SECTION 1
INTRODUCTION

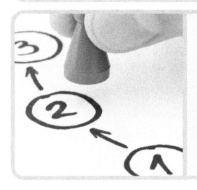

- How to Use This Book

- Why Sexuality Education?

- Misbeliefs and Facts About Sexuality and Persons with Developmental Disabilities

Human sexuality refers to a broad and complex spectrum of experiences and issues, not only the physical act of intercourse.

In the fall of 1985, several adolescent girls with intellectual disabilities who had experienced sexual abuse or who were considered to be at high risk for abuse came to our attention at the Waisman Center University Center for Excellence in Developmental Disabilities (UCEDD), University of Wisconsin-Madison. In getting to know these eight girls, we discovered some common themes: self-doubt, non-assertiveness, loneliness, sadness about being "different," and confusion and discomfort about matters related to sexuality. These young women, who had all been through puberty, were surprisingly lacking in basic information about their anatomy and unique female body functions. We recognized, though, that these young women were also curious, social, eager to learn, and in desire for friendships and other relationships. We attempted to link these girls with a community service that would meet their individual needs related to sexuality and abuse prevention but found none. The question, "Whose business is it?" would be one we would ask often. Believing in the need to create a resource where none exists, we began to make it our business.

From the start of our work, we realized the need for a clear definition of the term "human sexuality." Our definition of the term *human sexuality*: a broad and complex spectrum of experiences and issues including the person's self-concept, sexual identity, sexual body functions, social interactions with the same or opposite sex, values and beliefs, sexual expression including masturbation and intercourse, sexual health, and future planning. Although we were not experts in sexuality education or sexual abuse prevention when we began, as instructors in social work and nursing, we did have basic knowledge of human sexuality and experience working with persons with developmental disabilities. We also had a strong commitment to individual rights, including the rights of all persons to responsibly develop their sexuality and be safe from sexual abuse.

We continue to believe that with training and support, individuals with developmental disabilities can acquire the skills and knowledge necessary for developing a positive sexuality and reducing their risks for sexual abuse. This belief has been confirmed many times over the past twelve years. In this guidebook, we hope to share with you our experience so that together, we can make it our business to be part of the solution rather than part of the problem.

HOW TO USE THIS BOOK

The purpose of this book is to share a model for teaching the concepts of human sexuality to people with developmental disabilities. The STARS model focuses on four content areas: Understanding Relationships, Social Interaction, Sexual Awareness, and Assertiveness, with the goals of promoting positive sexuality and preventing sexual abuse. We provide assessment tools for identifying the strengths and needs of each person for learning and support in order to design an individualized training program. Goals and activities for each content area can be used to address these needs. This guidebook is intended for use by educators, social workers, nurses and other health care providers, psychologists, residential and vocational support persons, family members, and others interested in assisting and supporting individuals in this sensitive area.

"Prevention and education programs are important keys to reducing vulnerability to sexual abuse. Yet there is still a "hit or miss" approach by those traditionally charged with teaching sexuality."

— A case manager

The Activities

The activities in the guidebook are designed primarily for use with older teens and adults with mild/moderate developmental disabilities. Note: Refer to our publication, *STARS 2*, published by Future Horizons, Inc. for activities designed for youth in the primary grades through high school.

SECTION 1: INTRODUCTION

This book is to be used as an instructional guide rather than a packaged curriculum, and instructors are encouraged to figure out which activities are most suitable, to make adaptations to meet the participants' individual needs, and to enhance the training session with creative ideas.

Group or Individual

Most of the material in this book was developed out of our work with groups, but we find that many of the activities and ideas can be used or easily adapted for individual training as well. Individual training may be preferred for persons who do not learn well in a group or who do not desire a group experience, or when there are no resources available to support a group. For most people, though, the advantages of participating in a group are significant. A group experience provides the opportunity for practicing social skills, peer modeling ,and coaching, as well as the opportunity to meet new people and friends.

> For people with severe disabilities, who have limited capacity to learn self-protective behaviors, we believe that the ultimate responsibility for ensuring their safety and protection of personal safety needs to be assumed by trustworthy and sensitive caregivers.

Why Sexuality Education?

Sexuality is an important part of the total life experiences of human beings. Not surprisingly, people with developmental disabilities have sexual feelings, needs, and experiences. As with most people, their sexual desires are often linked with needs for closeness, caring, and emotional intimacy with others. People with developmental disabilities have unique learning needs in many aspects of their lives—sexuality is no exception. Individualized guidance and education for promoting positive sexuality and the prevention of sexual abuse is essential.

Human sexuality encompasses a broad and complex spectrum of experiences and issues including the individual's self-concept; sexual identity; sexual body functions; social interactions with others, sexual expression, including masturbation and intercourse; sexual health; and future planning. For most of us, sexuality education has been haphazard at best, with some coming from our parents, much more coming from our peers, and the rest coming from one or two classes in school and messages of all kinds from the media. For people with disabilities, opportunities for gaining accurate knowledge about sexuality may be even more limited. Family members, community support providers, and others who support people with disabilities may be unsure of how much

3

sexuality education to offer; they may be embarrassed to talk about sexuality, or they don't know how. As a result, many people with developmental disabilities lack basic sexual knowledge, are easily manipulated by others, and lack guidelines for the expression of sexual feelings.

> "However much we are cut off or sheltered from sex, however paralyzed or deformed we are, our sexual needs are the same as others."
>
> — Gunnel Enby, author with cerebral palsy, *Let There Be Love*

It is important to teach people with disabilities appropriate information about human sexuality as well as sexual expression that fits their developmental needs. For people with severe disabilities who have limited capacity to learn self-protective behaviors, we believe that the ultimate responsibility for ensuring their safety and protection of personal rights needs to be assumed by trustworthy and sensitive caregivers. With today's emphasis on community inclusion, it is essential that we include comprehensive sexuality education and abuse prevention training in our support services. By providing appropriate education, training, and support, it will be possible for people with developmental disabilities to develop the knowledge and skills necessary to engage in satisfying relationships and to acquire the protective behaviors necessary to move safely in society.

Misbeliefs and Facts About Sexuality and Persons with Developmental Disabilities

Misbeliefs and misunderstandings about sexuality and people with disabilities can unnecessarily and drastically inhibit the sexual expression of people with disabilities. Misconceptions can also affect other areas of a person's life, including self-esteem, vocational performance, and motivation to live as independently as possible. Misbeliefs need to be dispelled, and correct information needs to be provided.

Misbeliefs Regarding Sexuality

➤ People with developmental disabilities do not have sexual feelings/are asexual.

➤ People with developmental disabilities are over-sexed and have uncontrollable urges.

➤ It is unnecessary to talk about sex/sexuality because people with disabilities won't understand it, won't be able to cope with it emotionally, or won't have the opportunity.

SECTION 1: INTRODUCTION

Facts Regarding Sexuality

> People with developmental disabilities have a range of sexual desires and means of expression similar to that of people without a disability.

> The more accurate information and social skills training that people with disabilities receive the more likely that their sexual behavior will adhere to the cultural norm.

Misbeliefs Regarding Sexual Abuse

People with developmental disabilities are not vulnerable to sexual assault because:

> People feel sorry for them or find them undesirable, so they will not hurt them.

> They spend their time in supervised or safe settings, so they are not exposed to dangerous or exploitative situations.

> They are not sexually active, so they are less vulnerable.

Facts Regarding Sexual Abuse

People with developmental disabilities may be more vulnerable to sexual assault for several reasons:

> They may lack basic knowledge about anatomy, intercourse (and other sexual activities), reproduction, and sexually transmitted infections.

> They may lack information/education about sexual abuse.

> They may have been socialized to be compliant and passive and often exhibit a strong desire to please.

> They generally do not enjoy the same rights, privileges, and opportunities for privacy and normal healthy sexual relationships that most adults do.

The exploitation and misuse of accepted power relationships is a highly significant aspect of sexual assault. Offenders may think it is safer to assault someone with a disability because they perceive the individual as unable to defend themselves, unable to understand what is happening, and unable to report the incident or to be believed if he or she does report it.

An individual with a developmental disability may live, work, or spend leisure time in unsafe environments. A setting can be unsafe due to location, the structure, or occupants.

SECTION 2
THE STARS MODEL

- Content Areas and Goals
- Assessing the Needs of the Individual or "Figuring Out What to Teach"
- Guidelines for Support
- Involvement of Significant Others
- Guidelines for Training
- Policy Implications for Service Providers

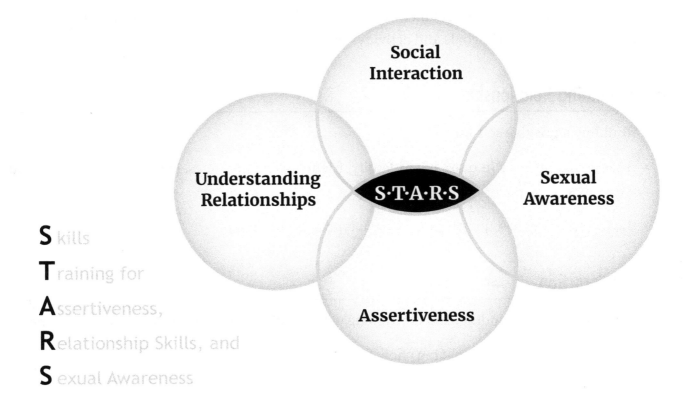

S kills
T raining for
A ssertiveness,
R elationship Skills, and
S exual Awareness

CONTENT AREAS AND GOALS

The STARS model originated through our efforts to design a training program for teaching basic personal safety skills to avoid sexual abuse. As we began working with individuals, we quickly learned that the issues of sexual abuse were connected to other issues, such as the person's self-esteem, assertiveness, understanding of sexuality, and opportunities to develop healthy relationships.

We recognized the need to teach and support positive expression of sexuality, in addition to facilitating the learning of skills to prevent sexual abuse. Equally important to consider in our work were the environments in which people spent their time and the attitudes and values of family, teachers, caregivers, and the community's response at large. The realization of the complex issues that people were facing led us to develop our STARS model as a more comprehensive or holistic training model.

In our STARS model, we present a "building blocks" approach to training about the complex areas of sexuality and abuse prevention. Each content area offers concepts, which we then build upon in the next content area. For example, many of the activities in the Assertiveness section build upon content and behaviors acquired in all three of the other content areas. The STARS model has four content areas, with specific goals and activities in each:

Understanding Relationships

> Building a positive self-image.

> Identifying persons in one's life as family, friends, acquaintances, community helpers , and strangers.

> Learning behaviors appropriate for each type of relationship.

Social Interaction

> Approaching, responding, and conversing with people in different settings and situations.

> Expressing preferences, making choices.

- Building friendships.

- Engaging in more mature relationships.

- Recognizing options for relationships into adulthood.

- Recognizing the components and responsibilities of a positive intimate relationship.

- Understanding the responsibilities of parenthood and the pros and cons of having children.

Sexual Awareness

- Building a positive self-image and sexual identity.

- Identifying gender.

- Identifying body parts and understanding their functions.

- Understanding public and private behavior.

- Differentiating between inappropriate and appropriate touching.

- Understanding the physical and emotional changes of puberty.

- Understanding sexual feelings and behaviors.

- Understanding reproduction.

- Examining personal and societal norms and values regarding sexual behavior.

- Learning about sexually transmitted infections.

- Discussing other health issues related to sexual awareness.

"The environments in which people with developmental disabilities live and work can highly influence their safety and the choices and options available for expression of sexuality and for the development of meaningful relationships."

— A sexuality educator

Assertiveness

- ➤ Increasing self-empowerment through words and actions.

- ➤ Recognizing a situation as potentially unsafe.

- ➤ Learning to say "no" and to use basic self-protection skills.

- ➤ Knowing how and where to get help at home and in the community.

- ➤ Reporting sexual harassment or assault.

ASSESSING THE NEEDS OF THE INDIVIDUAL OR "FIGURING OUT WHAT TO TEACH"

Family members and support providers often wonder when, what, and how to teach about sexuality to people with disabilities. Before beginning training, it is important to assess each person's current knowledge, skills, and attitudes in the four content areas of the STARS model.

Assessment Tools

In order to learn more about the individuals, we developed two assessment tools for this purpose, which are included in the Assessment section of this guidebook. The first, the "Sexual Attitudes and Knowledge (S.A.K.) Assessment," is used to assess the participant's current knowledge and attitudes about sexuality and sexual abuse prevention. The second, the "Sexual Abuse Risk Assessment (S.A.R.A.)," is used to assess the person's life settings and relationship network for purposes of identifying factors and situations which may be increasing the person's risk for sexual abuse.

Interviews

Along with use of the two assessment tools, interviews with the participant and significant others are also recommended. In gathering information, consider the following:

SECTION 2: THE STARS MODEL

1. What was the influence of a person's past experiences on their sexual attitudes, behaviors, and beliefs? Does the person come from a family environment in which sexuality was supported in positive ways? Or was there discomfort with the subject of sexuality?

2. What are the influences in the individual's current environment that may have an impact on the person's sense of themselves as a sexual being, such as caregiver attitudes and beliefs, social opportunities, and social rules?

3. The level of knowledge and experience related to sexuality and sexual abuse prevention may vary greatly for each individual, even for participants who are older adolescents and adults. Make no assumptions.

4. What is the individual's chronologic age? Social maturity? Cognitive ability? Incongruities might exist between the person's chronological age, social maturity, and physical development. For example, a nineteen-year-old person who is fully physically developed but whose cognitive abilities are more like a third-grader's will need to have information adapted and presented at a level that the person can understand.

5. Does the individual have any significant sensory differences, such as visual or hearing impairments, differences in tolerating noise or touch, or difficulties with self-regulation?

6. What are the person's communication abilities? Does the person communicate verbally or with other augmentative communication (e.g. computer, pictures etc.)?

7. What is the person's learning style?

8. Are there any specific needs or concerns relating to sexuality that need to be addressed? Think about this in a comprehensive way. Here are just a few examples:

   ❑ Is the person interested in dating?

   ❑ Has the person had difficulties with sexually inappropriate interactions with others?

   ❑ Or with inappropriate behaviors in public, such as masturbation?

   ❑ Has the person been sexually assaulted? (If so, consider whether specific counseling from a mental health counselor might be necessary in addition to teaching sexuality information.)

Individual Training Plan

The results of the two assessments, along with the interviews with the participant and significant others, can be used to determine where to focus training and support for each individual. Use the "Individual Training Plan" (included in the Assessment section) for each participant to record:

- strengths and concerns,

- plans for focusing the training, support, and intervention; and

- identification of the persons responsible for carrying out the training.

GUIDELINES FOR SUPPORT

To be effective in providing support around sexuality, it is important to develop honest, open, and supportive relationships with the people with whom you are engaged. To do this, you need to develop your own personal comfort with the area of sexuality and with people who have developmental disabilities. If there are areas of sexuality that you find challenging to communicate with others about, look for someone else to provide support around that specific area. Acceptance of individual difference with objectivity, naturalness, and empathy is extremely important. Group participants will likely sense the feelings and attitudes of the instructor and, even if not explicitly expressed, may internalize these beliefs. We have learned that if the instructor generates enthusiasm and conveys empathy, warmth, naturalness, and comfort, then a positive relationship is more likely to develop with the participants. To develop personal comfort and enhance group communication, it is helpful to consider the following principles:

- Examine your own attitudes about sexuality in general, and about sexuality and disability.

- Foster a positive attitude about sexual feelings when providing sexuality information. The goal is to promote healthy sexuality and safety, not to eliminate sexual responses.

- Work toward becoming an "askable" adult regarding sexuality. Promote a positive atmosphere for learning by being flexible, honest, and direct in manner and speech.

> Listen carefully to everything a person says; listen toward understanding. Avoid being critical or overly judgmental so those participants feel they can share ideas and ask questions without fear or punishment.

> Acknowledge every individual's right to knowledge, privacy, and sexual expression based on personal orientation and decision, and advocate for this right.

> Be aware of the wide variety of behaviors, values, attitudes, and feelings related to sexuality, and deal with them in a sensitive manner.

> Provide accurate information about sexuality. Even if a person never asks any questions about sexuality, realize that the person has already acquired some information from other sources and needs to know that you will clear up misconceptions, distortions, and fantasies. Provide straightforward, correct information, and check the person's understanding in a supportive manner.

Promote a positive atmosphere for learning by being flexible, honest, and direct in manner and speech.

> Recognize that teaching a person about sexuality will not lead the person to sexually acting out behaviors. Instead, understand that providing accurate information in clear-cut terms about sexual feelings and physical aspects of sexuality will reduce confusion and minimize the risk of inappropriate behavior and vulnerability.

> Keep a sense of humor while remaining respectful.

> Recognize that teaching and supporting individuals about sexuality can be risk-taking and stressful. Often a network of support, even one or two others whom you can trust to be supportive, can help you in coping with the stresses of providing education and support in this sensitive area.

INVOLVEMENT OF SIGNIFICANT OTHERS

As we help people with developmental disabilities develop skills for a desirable life, an important part of this training includes a focus on skills related to self-protection and the expression of positive sexuality. Within the individual's support network, a variety of persons, perhaps paid service providers, family members, or legal guardians, may be willing to take responsibility for ensuring these issues are addressed. To provide the most effective support, significant others need to be comfortable and knowledgeable in educating and/or responding to the person in regard to sexuality. Information and training to increase comfort and knowledge about human sexuality may be necessary and beneficial for these supportive individuals. The determination of which and how many significant others need to be involved in the training must be balanced between the individual's need for support and her/his rights of privacy and confidentiality.

We recommend that, prior to the start of the training program, you share information about the content and teaching methods with significant others. This allows time for questions and concerns to be shared and an opportunity to involve significant others in the training program. Sharing information can be done in a group or with individuals.

Many people wonder how sexuality training is received by the significant others in a participant's life. Generally, our experience has been that most significant others realize that information on sexuality and the prevention of sexual abuse is vital for the person for whom they advocate. Most have welcomed our assistance in these sensitive areas and have been supportive to us in carrying out the goals of the training program. We have encountered a few people who were either uncomfortable with the idea of a sexuality training program or who withdrew the participant once the group got started. Some were not opposed to the training in general but were uncomfortable with specific content. In these situations, we discussed concerns, provided information about specific components of the program, and came to an agreement about the individual's level of participation in the group. For people who were uncomfortable with the idea of a sexuality training program, sometimes we presented concerns in a non-threatening way about sexual abuse prevention and emphasized the importance of safety for the individual. Often, this opened the dialogue to other issues about sexuality education.

GUIDELINES FOR TRAINING

Group or Individual Learning

Most of the material in this book was developed out of our work with groups, but we find that many of the activities and ideas can be used or easily adapted for individual training as well. Individual training may be preferred for persons who do not learn well in a group or who do not desire a group experience, or when there are no resources available to support a group. For most people, though, the advantages of participating in a group are significant. A group experience provides the opportunity for practicing social skills, peer modeling, and coaching, as well as the opportunity to meet new people and friends.

Facilitators

Learning in groups occurs most effectively when facilitated by at least two trainers. Co-facilitation is important to provide support to each other, to allow for adequate support to participation, and to monitor group dynamics. For co-educational groups, including both a male and female facilitator works best. It is important for facilitators to encourage active participation of all individuals. The instructors serve as models for the rest of the group by encouraging and listening carefully to each group member. Members who are less vocal are encouraged to participate. If concepts are raised that are not relevant to the topic, respectful acceptance and gentle redirection is important. Each participant is reinforced for their efforts to contribute to the group.

Working with a Group: Selecting Participants

Who?

The original STARS activities were designed primarily for group work with older teens and adults with mild/moderate developmental disabilities.

Mixed-gender groups?

Groups can be of mixed genders or organized separately for specific genders. We have found that groups with mixed genders emulate the "real world" for most people. Mixed-gender groups enhance roleplaying and other activities, as well as fostering an appreciation for human development and sexuality issues of all genders. The content area and/or the comfort level of the instructor may influence whether the instruction is done for a mixed gender group. Sometimes participants may feel more comfortable learning some content separately, or the facilitator may be more at ease presenting gender-sensitive issues in same gender groups. If the facilitator is comfortable, even gender-sensitive issues like menstruation and condom use can be taught and discussed in a mixed-gender group. For example, all genders can benefit from learning about and handling menstrual hygiene products or condoms. Then, some of the more explicit discussion and demonstration about their use may be best done with same gender groups.

Number of participants in the group?

We recommend that the size of the group be small (four to eight members), so that the ratio of participants to facilitators will be about 2 or 3 to 1. Size will depend on individual needs of the participants, learning styles, and capacity of group leaders.

Individuals with any type of disability?

People who have mild or moderate intellectual disabilities, physical disabilities (such as cerebral palsy), hearing impairment, visual impairment, or behavioral challenges can participate in the groups. Consider whether a person will benefit from group participation. If the person has difficulty with disruptive behaviors when in a group setting, consider what types of support would be best so that the person can benefit from participation and so that others are not prevented from learning. Of course, needs must be individually assessed for each participant and training techniques modified accordingly.

Number & Frequency of Teaching Sessions

Sessions can be offered once a week for ten weeks and run approximately ninety minutes each with a break. Other options include holding forty-five-minute sessions two times weekly for ten weeks. Information should be shared at a pace that is comfortable for the group or individual. The pace will vary with the capabilities, attention span, and learning style of the individual.

Sharing Information

Share information about your program with participants and significant others prior to beginning the training program. Help them understand the importance of the program, provide detailed information about the content and teaching methods, and obtain the support of significant others whenever possible. Some instructors offer to meet with significant others individually (with the permission of the participant) to review the content of the program and to promote continuity and reinforcement of the training in the home environment. A sample letter about the sexuality training program is included in the Appendix.

Selecting Content for Teaching

This book is to be used as an instructional guide rather than a packaged curriculum, and support providers are encouraged to decide the individual needs of the participants and to enhance the training session with creative ideas. Based on the Assessment Tools and Interview information collected about each person, select content and activities from this original STARS guidebook that have been identified as areas of need for the participants. (Refer to the section Assessing the Needs of the Individual or "Figuring Out What to Teach" for details.) Choose content, which will effectively reach the participants and address issues relevant to their daily lives. When choosing content and activities, recognize that incongruities might exist between a person's chronological age, social maturity, and physical development.

For example:

> Consider a woman who is twenty-two years old, who is fully developed physically, and who has a moderate cognitive disability. She has been fully included in community life with residential and vocational support, and she has opportunities for many social experiences. Due to her intellectual disability, she has a very limited reading ability and difficulty with problem solving and judgment.

> Consider a young man who is seventeen years old, who has Asperger's Syndrome, and who is physically mature. He has above-average cognitive abilities, but he lacks awareness of the social world, and he has limited skills for social interaction. His parents would especially like him to understand social relationships and appropriate behaviors so that he will be less vulnerable to sexual abuse.

The information and skills that both people need is very similar to those needed by other people their age, but the information provided to them will need to be adapted for their unique learning needs.

Instructional Methods

The method of training is as important as the content of training. Generally, the information about sexuality that is appropriate for people with disabilities will be the same information as for other people without disabilities. Any information that you share with an individual person must be presented with the methods that are best for teaching the person. For example, it might be helpful to break the content down into the simplest concepts, use simple language, or use visual aids such as pictures or drawings.

Use a multi-sensory approach

We suggest that a variety of instructional methods be used. These methods include individual and group instruction, simple workbook activities, art, group discussion, audiovisual presentations, and role-playing. Anatomical dolls, photographs, and line drawings are the effective methods for identifying reproductive body parts and describing body functions and transmission of sexually transmitted infections. Group discussion, question and answer sessions, and storytelling are the most effective techniques for problem solving. Social skills are best taught through "real life practice" role-playing followed by group discussion. Lecturing is the least effective method because the group members may lose interest if not actively engaged. Examples of instructional methods:

> For visual learners, consider using *The Social Skills Picture Book for High School and Beyond* by Jed Baker, published by Future Horizons, Inc. This book includes a visual learning format for learning social skills that apply to real-life situations. The skills depicted are meant to be read, role-played, corrected when necessary, role-played some more, and finally, to be

SECTION 2: THE STARS MODEL

practiced by the student in real-life social situations. A CD is available to be used with the book as a teaching tool.

> Consider using *The New Social Story Book Revised and Expanded 15th Anniversary Edition* by Carol Gray (2015), published by Future Horizons, Inc. Developed through the author's years of experience, the book provides strategically written stories to explain social situations in ways children and adults with autism understand while teaching social skills needed to be successful at home, at school, at work, and in the community. There is a new section specifically for young adults.

Use your own creative methods for teaching

We encourage enhancing your training sessions with your own creative ideas. For some activities in the guidebook, there are references to specific resources for teaching. Teaching can be just as effective, though, using your own tools that are creatively made using common materials and that are tailored to the group or individual needs.

Role-playing

Role-playing is a particularly effective technique because it involves active participation of the group members. It gives the participants an opportunity to try out and rehearse new behaviors and to identify and change inappropriate behaviors. Group members can take turns between acting and observing each other. The group facilitators often need to model and provide specific instructions and support to do the role-plays. The participants who are the observers can act as peer coaches and provide feedback to the role-players. This active participation provides an opportunity for everyone to learn the concepts portrayed in the role-plays. A potential drawback of role-playing is that, at times, role-plays can become too "real" for some participants. For example, when someone is acting out a situation where one person is angry, the participant may believe that the other person is genuinely angry. When role-playing a threatening situation, the participant may forget that they are acting and may become truly frightened. It is important to keep reminding group members that "this is only acting, or make-believe." Another drawback can be that role-players might get too caught up in the role they are playing, rather than focusing on learning the concepts being taught. If the group facilitators provide ongoing sensitive support and instruction during the role-plays, the participants are less likely to experience these drawbacks.

Activities in the Natural Setting

Participants benefit most from the training when time is spent in their natural settings reviewing content and practicing skills related to the sexuality education training program. If trainers are not available for this individual work, other persons in the participant's support network can carry out this training activity. This time can be used to practice and reinforce skills and knowledge covered in the group meeting and to focus on issues identified in the Individual Training plan. At the end of the Activities section for each of the four content areas, we have included Community and Informal Activities.

Periodically Reassess Learning

Periodically assess the progress of the individual or group, as well as the effectiveness of your instructional techniques. Do this by observing how well each participant can answer questions pertaining to the material (for example, accurately labeling body parts), how well they join in group discussions about content, or how they participate in role-plays. Note also how the group responds to different methods of instruction (for example, observing length of attention span, expressions of boredom, amount of fidgeting, and level of interest and enthusiasm) for determining the best teaching techniques. Modify content or teaching methods according to the needs, preferences, and skills of the participants and your observations of their participation. The "Sexual Attitudes and Knowledge Assessment" tool may be used as a pretest and posttest to evaluate learning of group members.

Policy Implications for Service Providers

We find that the participants' behaviors and attitudes related to sexuality are influenced by service providers' policies regarding sexuality. The absence of a policy on sexuality also affects sexual expression. Adults with disabilities have the right to exercise their own choices and decision-making, and they have the right to social opportunities. These rights and opportunities, though, need to be balanced with safety concerns. Creative solutions can be found that both ensure safety and promote opportunity. For example,

> Adults with disabilities have the right to exercise their own choices and decision-making and they have the right to social opportunities.

when supporting individuals in dating situations, support can be provided similar to the concept of supported employment.

We encourage service providers to develop policies around sexuality and to make sure staff and consumers are aware of them. In the following excerpt from *The Right to Grow Up*, the author, Nancy Gardner, provides an excellent discussion of these issues. *[Note: Where appropriate, content in the excerpt has been updated to reflect current language usage, current philosophy, and practice.]*

> The key to successful programs is provision of whatever services a specific individual needs to "make it" in her or his community and to do so in a way that is as much like what everyone else does as possible. How "making it" is defined differs from culture to culture, town to town, family to family, even person to person. But some generalizations are possible. For example, almost everyone wants a comfortable home of his or her choosing; an enjoyable job that provides an adequate income to survive; and a loving, caring relationship with someone special, whether they are family, spouse, or friends.

> When setting up services for persons with developmental disabilities, these same cultural goals should be considered. Generally, programs should have specific policies that encourage adult dignity and respect for the sexuality of the persons served. All service providers should ask themselves whether their policies take the following factors into consideration: privacy, social opportunities, respect for choice and sexuality, safety, and protection of legal rights.

The rule of thumb for program policies should be to provide the same level of respect, privacy, and social opportunities that persons without disabilities expect in their own homes, workplaces, and communities.

Privacy

> - Does the person have a bedroom of their own? If not, are there "private places" where residents can go to be alone or interact with potential sexual partners?

> - If there is a shared bathroom, are there rules respecting each person's privacy when he or she uses it?

Social Opportunities

> Are there opportunities for social interaction that include integrated settings?

> Are transportation services available after 5 PM and on weekends?

> Are individuals given the opportunity to use cell phones and social media?

> Does social skills training include dating, and does the person have the option to date if he/she desires?

> Is the person provided with age-appropriate recreation and social activities?

Respect for Choice and Sexuality

> Are there rules regarding bedtime or can individuals choose their own bedtime?

> Are consumers given the opportunity to shop for their own clothes?

> Are adult women taught to purchase and use cosmetics?

> May consumers choose their own roommates and decide where and with whom they would like to go for recreational activities?

> Are staff given training and policy guidance to develop an accepting attitude and supportive approach regarding the sexual expression, gender identity, and sexual orientation of persons with disabilities?

> Can couples remain in the service program if they choose to marry?

> Are consumers given training in sexuality, birth control, avoidance of sexual exploitation, and interpersonal aspects of sexuality?

> Are there specific procedures and policies regarding correction of inappropriate sexual behavior?

> Are consumers provided with due process guarantees in regard to any training programs? Are staff and parents given information about laws and policies, and medical and psychological consequences of sterilization?

➤ Are there procedures for reporting sexual abuse and policies relating to staff or others who may be involved?

Unfortunately, many programs have practices and patronizing policies that would be unthinkable for nondisabled persons. As much as possible, the rule of thumb for program policies should be to provide the same kind of respect, privacy, and social opportunities that persons without disabilities expect in their own homes, workplaces, and communities.

Reprinted with permission from Nancy Gardner, "Sexuality," in The Right to Grow Up, *ed. Jean Ann (Baltimore: Paul H. Brookes Publishing Co., Inc., 1986).*

SECTION 3
UNDERSTANDING RELATIONSHIPS

- Building a Positive Self-Image

- Identifying Persons in One's Life as Relatives, Friends, Acquaintances, Community Helpers, and Strangers

- Learning Behaviors Appropriate for Each Type of Relationship

While most of us choose with whom we will live, work, and spend our leisure time, people with developmental disabilities often have little opportunity to make these choices.

Except for the hermit on the mountain, we all live our daily lives in a network of relationships. Societal trends—such as population mobility, social media, blended families, and the inclusion of people with disabilities into settings with people who do not have disabilities—have increased the variety of people with whom individuals relate. The individual's understanding of the various types of relationships in their network directs and influences their interactions and behaviors. The ability to identify people as family members, intimate and close friends, acquaintances, community helpers, and strangers is based on several abstract concepts. Developing an understanding of relationships and the norms of behavior and social interaction is a key component for adolescents and adults with disabilities to build satisfying relationships and protect themselves from abusive situations. To develop an understanding of these abstract concepts, many people with disabilities need direct instruction and practice.

When teaching this content area, it is important to remember several factors that often affect the lives of persons with developmental disabilities. While most of us choose the people with whom we will live, work, and spend our leisure time, people with developmental disabilities often have little opportunity to make these choices. They may rarely have the opportunity to be with family members or develop social and intimate relationships. They often share personal living space and experience daily life in relationships with people that have been arranged by others. Fortunately, for many, these arranged relationships evolve into friendships or an alternative family. Many persons with developmental disabilities have a tenuous relationship network due to high staff turnover or frequent change of environments. This lack of continuity of relationships can be very stressful. Staff members often fulfill multiple roles, including counselor, supervisor, or friend. Not surprisingly, many people with developmental disabilities experience confusion when defining their relationships with staff. In the role of "client," many adults with developmental disabilities have relationships with their families and service providers characterized by an imbalance of power. Whether real or perceived, this imbalance affects the feelings and behaviors associated with the relationship, often resulting in a diminished sense of self.

Having positive relationships is at the core of our feelings of well-being. It is important to focus our efforts on expanding social networks and promoting opportunities for meaningful relationships to develop. Supporting relationships may be the most important investment we make toward improving the quality of life for people with developmental disabilities.

GOAL 1: Building a Positive Self-Image

Activities:

1. Get acquainted. Put a large sheet on the wall for each participant. Write a group member's name at the top of each page and ask the person to respond to simple questions such as:

   ➤ What is your favorite food?

   ➤ What sports or activities do you like?

   ➤ Where would you like to go on vacation?

Continue for each group member. Point out common interests, as well as individual differences between group members. (See Example A, MY LIKES, page 34).

2. Group sharing. At the beginning of each meeting, give each person an opportunity to tell something of importance or interest that occurred during the week. It can be personal (for

example, "I have a new boyfriend") or general (for example, "I got a new job"). Use this time to build group rapport. Acknowledge and accept all comments. If someone brings up something too sensitive for group sharing, tell him or her so and suggest they talk with you or a support person in private.

3. Have each person think about when she/he/themselves is proud of or pleased with himself/ herself/themselves. Each person in turn can complete the sentence, "I am proud of myself when..."

4. Share with individuals that how we feel about ourselves involves both things we can see on the "outside" and things in our mind or "inside." List things we can see on the outside (our physical appearance), and things in our mind or inside (our beliefs and feelings).

5. Make a booklet in the shape of a male or female with lines for writing. Note: there may be variations on the person's shape when the person is transgender. On the front or "outside," have participants list the things people can see which they like about themselves (physical self). On the "inside" of the book, list things they like about themselves which can't be seen (emotional self; cheerful, honest, helpful, friendly.)

6. Sitting in a circle, take turns having group members look at the person on their right and say something they like or find attractive about the person. This activity builds self-esteem, provides an opportunity to express opinions, and establishes a good time to practice accepting compliments in a gracious manner (saying "thank you" instead of giggling).

7. Using a full-length mirror, encourage each group member to look at his or her whole body. This helps the person with disabilities develop a concept and acceptance of their body boundaries and appearance.

GOAL 2: Identifying Persons in One's Life as Relatives, Friends, Acquaintances, Community Helpers, and Strangers

Before beginning this section, assist the individual in gathering information about their network of relationships. Note: this information may have been collected using the Sexual Abuse Risks Assessment (S.A.R.A.), which is included in the Appendix.

Activities:

1. Make a poster for each person by using a separate, large piece of paper and pasting a photograph or drawing a picture and writing the name of the person at the top of the page. In turn, assist each person to write names of family members, co-workers, neighbors, community helpers, etc.

2. For teaching about social relationships, rules, and behavior, we suggest using a relationship map such as the "CIRCLES" program (see Appendix for information about this resource) or a drawing of concentric circles on a paper (example below). This is a teaching tool that is designed to assist individuals who have difficulty learning the abstract concepts of personal space, social distance, and appropriate social and sexual behavior. It can be used to teach social distance and levels of familiarity using concentric circles.

Relationship Map

Strangers

Community Helpers

Friends

Family

Self

2. (cont.) To use the Relationships Map, give each participant a paper with the circles identified with different types of relationships (self, family, friends, acquaintances, community helpers, and strangers.) Assist participants in identifying where to place people who are in their social network within the circles. Some people find it helpful to put names of people in each circle.

3. "What is a family?" Discuss all types of families (e.g., families headed by two parents, single parents, grandparents raising children, and same-sex parents). Some families are not biologically related, such as adoptive or foster families. Provide an opportunity for participants to share family photos or information about their own families.

Family

4. Group discussion: "Who are your friends?" and "What is a friend?" Ask participants to name a friend and tell why that person is a friend. List, on a wall poster, reasons why we call people friends, such as "help each other." The focus here is on understanding who our friends are and what friendship means. See Goal #1: Approaching, Responding to…Situations, page 26, in "Section Four: Social Interaction," for activities related to how to make and socialize with friends.

Friends

5. Discuss other aspects of friendship. Points to emphasize:

   ➤ Differences between a close friend and a casual friend.

   ➤ Friendships often take time to develop. Have group members discuss any longtime friends.

   ➤ Friends may not get along every day.

   ➤ Friends change and it is "okay" to stop being friends if a relationship feels bad most of the time.

   ➤ This is a good time to discuss social media, including positive opportunities for meeting new friends and the potentially negative and scary aspects of connecting with harmful individuals. See the Appendix: Resources section for more detailed references and guidance about safety and social media.

Romantic Relationships

6. Discuss "romantic" relationships. Share that people sometimes have friendships that develop into romantic relationships. In a romantic relationship, a person has special feelings for someone else, and it is known as "being in love." Ask the participants if they know people who are in love or if they have been in love with another person.

Strangers

7. Talk about strangers. Help group members identify who is or is not a stranger. Ask participants, by naming specific friends, family, and acquaintances, as well as strangers, to discriminate people they "know" from those they "don't know." For example, "Is the garbage collector a stranger? Is the librarian at the public library a stranger?" Review why people are or are not strangers.

Community Helpers

8. Discuss types of strangers (people whom you do not know and whose names you do not know).

   ➤ Safe strangers. These may include:

      ❑ Community helpers you could ask for help in an emergency, such as police, firefighters, mail carriers, and nurses; and

      ❑ Other people who live in our community, such as salesclerks, restaurant workers, or security guards.

Dangerous Strangers

   ➤ Dangerous strangers. These include people who want to harm others and from whom you want to protect yourself. Identify clues that indicate that someone may be dangerous.

   Include examples such as:

      ❑ A stranger asks you to go somewhere or to get into their car.

      ❑ A stranger offers to pay you money or give you a present if you do something that doesn't seem right.

      ❑ Someone you meet on the internet asks you for personal information or to meet in person.

9. Help participants use their intuition or "gut feelings" to identify possible dangerous or unsafe situations at home or in the community. Sometimes strangers hurt us, but other times even people we know may hurt us (for example, touching our private parts or asking us to do something scary that we don't want to do, like touching their private parts). Discuss how your body feels when you are afraid or scared (for example, heart pounds, breaths quicken, hands sweat). This means your body is telling you that something isn't right. Group members need to learn to respond to these feelings. Tell them not to talk to the person but to get away from the person and tell someone. Protective behavior skills are more fully discussed in the section on Assertiveness.

10. Emphasize that most strangers will not harm you and that there are clues you can use (see Goal #2: Identifying Persons in One's Life as Relatives... and Strangers, Activity #9, page 31 for this concept) and "gut" feelings to help you tell if someone is dangerous.

GOAL 3: Learning Behaviors Appropriate for Each Type of Relationship

Activities:

1. Use posters made earlier for each group member (see Goal #2: Identifying Persons in One's Life as Relatives...and Strangers, Activity #1, page 28, to review the people in their lives with their corresponding relationships. Identify the behaviors and patterns of interaction that are appropriate with each type of relationship and write the appropriate behavior under each relationship (See Example B, GREETINGS, page 35.)

Greeting Others

2. Using the Relationship Map made earlier (see Goal #2: Identifying Persons in One's Life as Relatives...and Strangers, Activity #2, page 28) to review the types of relationships and identify the social behavior that is

Relating Actions to Relationships

appropriate for each. It may be helpful to identify specific behaviors for specific people in the person's life. For example:

> ➤ **Family Circle:** Family members are the people we're closest to. Family members can have hugs and kisses. We say "I love you" to family members. We can talk about private things with our parents.

> ➤ **Friend Circle:** To our closest friends, we can give hugs when we say hello and goodbye. We can say "I like you" to them.

> ➤ **Community people/helpers:** People in our classes or work places or neighbors can have a handshake and a wave. We can say, "Hello, how are you?" and smile.

> ➤ **Strangers:** Strangers are people we have not met and don't know. We can be polite and say, "Thank you," and "Excuse me," if we need to. But otherwise we don't talk to strangers.

Encourage the participants to use their Relationship map in all environments in which they spend time to identify social relationships and appropriate behaviors.

3. "Is It OK?" Game. Read aloud the questions below about social behavior. Have participants respond to statements by holding up either a card which has OK or a card with NOT OK for each one. For example:

> ➤ Is it OK to hug your mother?

> ➤ Is it OK to kiss your boss?

> ➤ Is it OK to kiss the store clerk?

> ➤ Is it OK to hug someone you just met?

> ➤ Is it OK to wave to a stranger?

> ➤ Is it OK to give personal information to someone over the internet?

Review these concepts in a discussion. Acknowledge that behavior sometimes depends on circumstances of where and when the interaction is taking place.

4. Role-play each different greeting used when meeting a friend, relative, co-worker, employer, or acquaintance.

5. On a large sheet of paper write down different behaviors such as kissing, hugging, shaking hands, and waving. Ask participants to list the people it would be all right to interact with in this way (for example, mother, boyfriend). Continue listing people for each behavior (see Example D, WHO WOULD YOU...? page 28).

Community or Informal Activities:

1. There are many opportunities to foster self-esteem on a daily basis in natural settings. Encourage participants and significant others to say something they like about the other person, such as "You have a nice haircut."

2. Peer groups can be encouraged to reinforce each other. For example, they can do so by clapping for each other's successes or making comments to each other using "I like it when you..." statements.

3. While in the community, ask the person to identify community helpers. Include "safe" people such as bus drivers, store clerks, and teachers who might be approached if help is needed. Point out that police are not always around and it is important to identify who may be other "safe" people.

4. With the group member, look at his/her photo album. Identify specific people and discuss various types of relationships.

5. Watch a favorite TV show or movie together, identifying relationships between the characters in the show and talking about whether the behavior is "OK" or not.

Understanding Relationships – Activity Examples

EXAMPLE A
My Likes—by Mark   Pizza, Summer, Bowling, Hawaii

EXAMPLE B
Mark's Relationships   Paste photo or write name of each person.

Joan – Mom	Mike – Best Friend
Ellen - Neighbor	Susan – Job Coach

SECTION 3: UNDERSTANDING RELATIONSHIPS

EXAMPLE C

Greetings

Paste photo or write name of each person.

Joan – Mom – "Mom Kiss"	Mike – Best Friend – Hug

Ellen – Neighbor – Wave	Susan – Job Coach – Shake Hands or Fist Bump

EXAMPLE D

Who would you...?

Kiss	➔	Parents, boyfriend
Shake hands	➔	Someone being introduced to you
Hug	➔	Good friend, family member
Wave at	➔	Neighbor, child

SECTION 4
SOCIAL INTERACTION

- Approaching, Responding to, and Conversing with People in Different Settings and Situations

- Expressing Preferences, Making Choices

- Building Friendships

- Engaging in More Mature Relationships

- Recognizing Options for Relationships Into Adulthood

- Recognizing the Components and Responsibilities of a Positive Intimate Relationship

- Understanding the Responsibilities of Parenthood and the Pros and Cons of Having Children

"A Story"

We were strangers in her first year. Then we met. Then she transferred, same year. We met together. Closer. Did things. What would you like to do today? Let's go bowling. We planned it together. We held hands, hugged a lot. Because we were friends. As best friends. — Robert

SOCIAL INTERACTION

The opportunity for social interaction is important to all of us. To interact effectively with others, we learn how to approach people and respond to people in ways acceptable to our culture. As we are socialized, we learn to express our needs, preferences, and opinions, how to give and get information, and how to make friends and develop intimate relationships.

As people with disabilities become more involved in community life, we realize that the need for social skills training is as important as instruction in cooking, money management, housekeeping, or shopping. Social skills are often acknowledged as important yet given low priority when individual learning goals are written and carried out. As a result, many people lack the skills to effectively communicate their feelings and wishes and to relate to others without guidance and support. Some people may develop inappropriate or anti-social behaviors that jeopardize their participation in educational and vocational programs. In addition, the style of social engagement of persons with disabilities, such as autism or Asperger's, may be misinterpreted.

Social adjustment is closely linked to self-esteem. Years of isolation, limited participation in community life, and feelings of failure have left many adults with poor self-concepts and difficulty relating to others. With this generation, we believe there is much we can do to prevent and counteract the ill effects of labels and limited opportunities. It begins with helping young people to see themselves as attractive human beings, appreciate their gifts and talents, and develop a positive vision of themselves in the future.

A person's self-concept is enhanced by opportunities to make choices, express preferences, and give opinions. Many people with disabilities need specialized support and "coaching" for understanding social rules and developing socially appropriate behaviors. Direct instruction in social skills, positive role modeling, and lots of opportunity for practice can greatly enhance social integration. Efforts to enhance social interaction should also be directed at helping others accept the person's behavior or verbalizations.

The goals and activities in this section build upon the participant's fundamental understanding of relationships and accompanying behaviors, which is covered in Section Three, Understanding Relationships. Social skills development in this area is excellent groundwork for the later section, Assertiveness.

GOAL 1: Approaching, Responding to, and Conversing with People in Different Settings and Situations

Activities:

1. Who and where would you...? On a large sheet of paper write the word *PARENT* or someone you may kiss. Then list several settings—home, grocery store, ball game, restaurant. Ask if it is acceptable to kiss in all of these places or why not, and what other factors might be important (your age, presence of others, type of activity going on). Continue the activity for other people, behaviors and settings, (see Example E, Who and Where Would You? page 35.) Discuss how behaviors or interactions differ according to the setting as well as the person.

   Relating
   Actions
   Settings

2. Identify facial expressions and feelings. Show participants' various facial expressions and label the feelings that go along with them (for example, angry, sad, and happy). Have group members make facial expressions also. Use of a mirror is helpful.

   Expressions

3. Role-play the expression of various feelings using words, signs, pictures, gestures, or expressions. For example, how would you express these feelings?

   Recognizing
   Feelings

   ➤ Sadness

   ➤ Anger

   ➤ Feeling sorry

   ➤ Love

   Note: If you are helping someone who uses augmentative communication modalities, be sure that their communication includes symbols, pictures, or phrases that reflect feelings and emotions.

Reading Nonverbal Messages

4. What is the Message? Role-play situations in which participants are asked to interpret nonverbal communication. For example, what is the message if the person:

   ➤ Smiles and nods their head? (Yes or okay)

   ➤ When greeting a person, extends arm and hand? (Wants to shake hands)

   ➤ Pulls body back when approached for hug? (Doesn't want to hug)

5. Role-plays. Once the group is comfortable with role-plays, ask them to suggest situations they would like to role-play. Here are examples to begin with:

   ➤ Meeting someone new at a party. Two people pretend to be at a party where they meet each other for the first time. Role-play introducing themselves to each other and making conversation. Point out the appropriate amount of information to reveal and topics of conversation with someone you are meeting for the first time.

   ➤ Conflict resolution. Two participants role-play coworkers who are having problems getting along with each other at work. Practice ways they can express their feelings to each other and resolve conflict.

GOAL 2: Expressing Preferences, Making Choices

Activities:

Expressing Preferences

1. Refer to Goal #1: Building a Positive Self-Image, Activity #1, in Section Three: Understanding Relationships, page 25 to help group members share interests and express preferences.

Making Decisions

2. Show the group three pieces of artwork. Ask each person which one he/she likes the most and why. Discuss individual preferences or tastes. Ask what opportunities participants have to make choices (for example, if they have choices in clothing, room decor, or activities).

3. Tell short stories in which the character must make a choice. Have each group make their own decision about what they would do and why. Examples of short stories:

   ➤ Cindy is planning to go bowling with friends. Her sister, Linda, calls and invites her to dinner the same night. What do you think she should do?

   ➤ Ron and his roommates are planning a picnic for Saturday. What do you think would be good to bring along to eat?

   ➤ Your coworkers have organized a swimming party and invite you to come. You would really like to go, but you feel embarrassed because you don't know how to swim. What are some of your choices? What would you choose to do?

   ➤ Your friend, John, tells you about a new social group forming, and he invites you to join. Discuss what things you might want to consider when making your decision (for example, the activities of the social group, the other group members attending, the time of the meetings, and transportation).

GOAL 3: Building Friendships

Activities:

1. For activities about building friendships, see Goal #2: Identifying Persons in One's Life as Family, Friends..., Activities #4 and #5, in Section Three: Understanding Relationships, page 25. As a group, create a list of characteristics to look for in a good friend. For example:

   Friendships

   ➤ Likes to have fun

   ➤ Likes to do things together

   ➤ Listens to you

> Really cares what happens to you

> Stands up for you

> Helps you when you are sick

2. Make a similar list of "Ways to Be a Good Friend."

Evolving Relationships

3. Use a Relationship Map, such as the one on page 28, or the CIRCLES program (see Appendix: Resources for details) to help individual students develop an understanding of how intimacy levels change as relationships change, such as with an acquaintance that becomes a close friend.

Enhancing Network of Relationships

4. Ask the group to think of someone that they would like to know better. Make a list of things they could do to become closer to the person. (See Example F, WAYS TO BECOME BETTER FRIENDS, page 51.) Role-play one or more of the suggestions.

5. Role-plays.

> Your friend feels bad. What could you say or do?

> Giving and receiving a gift.

> A co-worker asks you to go the movies. You don't feel like going out tonight, but you are interested in developing a friendship with the person. What could you say or do?

> Inviting a friend to visit your home.

Manners

6. Review etiquette and manners. For example:

> Saying good-bye.

> Taking turns in conversations.

> Saying "please" and "thank you."

> Role-play situations involving various social skills and table manners.

SECTION 4: SOCIAL INTERACTION

7. Host a "gourmet" meal with group members. Encourage participants to practice manners at a table set with linens, flowers, and candles. Go out to a "nice" restaurant. Practice ordering, using manners at the table and conversation during the meal.

GOAL 4: Engaging in More Mature Relationships

Activities:

1. Review the concept of "respect" as a necessary component in a good relationship. How do people show respect? How do you know someone respects you? Role-play showing respect.

   Respect

2. Discuss "romantic" relationships. Explain that teenagers and adults sometimes have friendships that develop into romantic relationships—like between a husband and wife or two people who are dating. In a romantic relationship, the person has special feelings for another, which are called being "in love." Ask participants if they know people who are in love, either in real life or in the movies or TV, or whether they have been in a romantic relationship.

   Romantic Relationship

3. What is love? Discuss the different types of love a person can have. For example, loving a pet, loving nature, loving people in your family, loving God, loving a good friend, married love (which can include being friends and sexual love).

   Love

4. What is the difference between "liking a person" and "loving a person"? Explain that the difference is related to how strong the feelings of affection and attraction are towards the other person. Have students draw someone or something they "like" and someone or something that they "love." Ask them to discuss their choices. Consider the following:

   ➤ If you are friends with someone, the relationship could just remain as a friendship, and you could become really "good friends."

43

> Sometimes when you meet or look at someone, you realize that you feel something besides friendship—you have "romantic" feelings. These feelings may turn into love—a really strong caring feeling. Love is more than physical attraction; a person's "inner qualities" are also important, and it takes time for love to develop. Also talk about strong attraction before you really get to know the person well; it might not be love, but "infatuation."

5. Discuss what happens when you think you care about someone:

   > Sometimes the other person will like you as much as you like them, or more, or less; or

   > Sometimes the other person will not be interested in a relationship with you; or

   > Sometimes your feelings could change (feelings get stronger or deeper, or less interested).

6. What do you look for in a boyfriend or girlfriend? Emphasize the "inner qualities" vs. the "outer" or surface qualities.

Dating

7. When people who have a romantic relationship go out together, it is called dating. Note that you can also have a "date" with someone who is just a friend. Discuss each aspect of the date, and then role-play or help the group members plan actual dates and rehearse.

   > Planning the date—where, when, transportation, phone number, address, cost.

   > Asking someone—by phone, in person.

   > Accepting/refusing a date.

   > Getting ready—hygiene, appropriate dress.

   > Behavior on the date—saying good night.

8. Refer to Section Five: Sexual Awareness for more content on dating behaviors, values, sexual Behavior, and reproductive health that are all part of mature relationships.

GOAL 5: Recognizing Options for Relationships into Adulthood

There are many options today for developing satisfying relationships in adulthood. All of us have the human need for feeling connected with other people, but this may come in different forms. Many people have connections with others that do not involve romantic relationships. It is important to help group members develop an awareness of the options available for them. Assist participants in considering which of the options would feel most satisfying for them. For some people, it might mean living with an adult foster family and having a few same-sex peers as close friends to share special activities. It might mean having a special opposite sex or same-sex romantic partner, perhaps headed toward living together and a more permanent relationship as in marriage, or not.

Activities

1. Help group members think about possible options for a desirable adult life. Recognize that in our diverse society, options for some people may be guided by cultures, values, and norms. Examples include living in an apartment, owning a house, having a job, having friends, and getting married. Take into consideration cultural or family influences on their choices. Encourage participants to think about what responsibilities each of these choices require and what type of support they need to accomplish their goals.

   Options for a Desirable Life

2. Create a story about independent or supported living. This may mean living alone, having a housemate, having a live-in caregiver, or living in a co-op. In the story, include the responsibilities of living independently and

   Responsibilities of Adult Life

managing a household. Include earning money, paying bills, doing household tasks, cooking, shopping, and using transportation. Help group members think about what type of support they need to carry out the tasks. An example of a story which might be used:

> Ralph moved into an apartment last month. To pay for his expenses, he has a job and he receives government benefits that he is qualified for because he has a developmental disability. His expenses include rent, food, phone bill, bus fare, and clothing. A support worker from the agency responsible for his residential placement stops by regularly after Ralph gets home from work to assist with food preparation, talk about Ralph's daily routine, and help in problem-solving Ralph's concerns and needs.

> List on a large sheet of paper or the blackboard the responsibilities in the story. If there are other things that Ralph would need to do in his household, list these too.

GOAL 6: Recognizing the Components and Responsibilities of a Positive Intimate Relationship

Activities

Identifying
Qualities
in Positive
Relationships

1. Review the concepts of friendships and the qualities of a positive relationship, using Goal #2: Identifying Persons in One's Life as Family...and Strangers, Activity #4, in Section Three: Understanding Relationships, page 25. Talk about the things outside (physical appearance) and the things inside (inner qualities) that make up a person. Remind participants that the "inner" qualities of a person are the most important to consider when deciding whether to have a relationship with someone and what kind of relationship it will be.

2. During group meeting, model, label, and reinforce behaviors and attitudes that promote friendship and relationship building.

3. Group discussion. Ask group participants for their ideas about the different stages or steps that two people go through together on their way to developing an intimate relationship and making a commitment to each other. It is important to acknowledge that there may be aspects of culture that need to be considered. For example, in certain cultural traditions, there are rules that women and girls must be accompanied on a date by a male family member.

Understanding Stages or Steps of Relationships

> ➤ These steps include: becoming friends, dating, asking yourself if this is the right person for you, courting, and asking yourself if this is the right time to make a serious commitment, marriage, or partnership.

> ➤ Emphasize that it is best if these steps take some time, rather than rushing into making a serious commitment. Help participants realize that on television and in the movies, couples seem to go through these steps or stages very quickly. But, in real life, it is better to get to know the person slowly and ask yourself each step of the way if this is the right person and decision for you.

> ➤ Review each of the steps. Talk about each step, listing it on a piece of large paper or on the blackboard. Underneath, list the specific activities that two people do in each step. For example, under "becoming friends" you might list, with the help of the participants, that you do things together and talk about things you have in common. Under "asking yourself if this is the right person for you," you might list, "identifying the inner qualities of the person."

> ➤ Discuss concepts with group members who may be in a particular stage of a relationship.

4. Role-play conflict resolution and problem solving. The ability to successfully resolve conflicts and solve problems when living with others requires the individual to avoid blaming, name-calling, making judgments, and telling the another person what to do. Group members will benefit from practicing positive problem-solving behaviors to reach a satisfying

Conflict Resolution

resolution. Have participants suggest specific problem situations they have experienced with others. Group members can role- play behaviors to solve the problem in a positive way, then role-play behaviors that would prevent a positive solution to the problem. Discuss problem-solving strategies.

Marriage

5. Group discussion about marriage. Ask group members some of the reasons why they think people get married. These reasons include love, companionship, sexual attraction, respect, mutual interest, mutual goals, mutual values, and ability to communicate and solve problems. Then continue the discussion with some of the wrong reasons for getting married: just wanting to have sex, "everyone is getting married," pressure from friends/family, avoiding problems at home, or pregnancy. Recognize that there may be participants for whom there are cultural differences related to marriage, such as arranged marriage.

Long-Term Commitment

6. Group discussion. Discuss positive reasons for making a long-term commitment. Review important aspects of a positive relationship. What does it feel like to love someone? How do people show love in different types of relationships? What do we mean by respect? How do people show respect in marriage? How do you know when your partner respects you?

Responsibilities of a Committed Relationship

7. Create a story about a couple. In the story, include the responsibilities of a committed relationship. Include the aspects of managing a household. Examples include earning money, sharing household tasks, cooking, shopping, finding time for recreation, and taking care of each other during sickness.

➤ Example: Alex and Heather got married six months ago and rented an apartment. To pay rent and all their other expenses, such as for food, the phone bill, and clothing, they both must have jobs in the community. Heather likes to get up early each morning. While Heather fixes breakfast, Alex makes lunches for each of them to carry to work. Alex and Heather ride the bus together. Heather gets off the bus first at her job, and she tells Alex she will see him in the afternoon. Alex gets off the bus at his job. After work, Alex and Heather ride the same bus home, and on some

SECTION 4: SOCIAL INTERACTION

days, they stop at the grocery store to buy groceries. On one day, Heather doesn't feel very well when they arrive home, so Ralph suggests that she go to bed, and he fixes soup for them both.

➤ List on a large sheet of paper or the blackboard the responsibilities for the couple in the story and list who did each activity. For example:

❑ Work in the community—both Heather and Alex
❑ Fix breakfast—Heather
❑ Grocery shopping—both Heather and Alex
❑ Fix supper—Alex

Identify and list other things that Heather and Alex would need to do in their relationship and in their household.

GOAL 7: Understanding the Responsibilities of Parenthood and the Pros and Cons of Having Children

Activities:

1. Discuss responsibilities of parenting a child. What must parents provide for a child in order to assure adequate care? Individually or in a group, discuss the need for housing, food, clothing, health care, childcare, toys, education, and discipline. What do parents need to do to provide these things for their children? Do the participants think that they are capable of raising children now, or ever? Talk about why and why not.

Responsibilities of Parenting

2. Role-play. Have two people take the roles of parent and young child. They role-play a situation in which the parent tries to find ways of getting the child to clean her room and the child does not want to do it. Afterwards, talk about the difficulty in getting the child to do the activity, and discuss what techniques the parent used to gain their child's cooperation. Be sure to reinforce positive parenting techniques.

49

3. Invite a young couple with a small child to share some of their experiences in learning about the responsibilities involved in marriage and starting a family.

4. Discuss other options besides parenting for interaction with children. Talk about roles, such as being an aunt/uncle and work or volunteer opportunities in a daycare setting or school. Remind individuals that, for safety of all, encourage adults with disabilities to get permission from the child's parent to interact with them and do so in the presence of a parent.

5. Realistic exposure to daily life with children is important. For example, visit a daycare center so that group members can observe and spend time with children.

Community or Informal Activities:

1. Encourage and provide opportunities for participants to make choices in their daily life (such as choosing activities, making purchases, picking out clothing, and deciding what to eat.) Making these choices gives individuals experience and preparation for making bigger decisions such as choosing friends or being sexual with another person.

2. Encourage participants to be involved in planning processes in which decisions are made about their own lives.

3. In natural settings, model, label, and reinforce behavior and attitudes with people who promote friendship and relationship building. Prompt or coach people when they seem confused.

4. When reading books or stories or watching TV or videos, point out examples of friendship and relationship building.

5. Some communities have developed "Personals" sections for persons with disabilities in safe, disability-aware publications, such as newsletters by disability advocacy groups. Placing or responding to "ads" can be a means of positive social networking. If a person is interested, help them write and/or respond to ads and be sure to review safety precautions.

SECTION 4: SOCIAL INTERACTION

Social Interactions – Activity Examples

EXAMPLE E
Who and Where would you...? Give your mother a "Mommy kiss"

Home	➜	Yes
Grocery Store	➜	No
Movies	➜	No
Picnic	➜	Maybe

EXAMPLE F
Ways to become friends

Eating lunch together

Inviting someone to my house or visiting their house

Talking to them on the phone after school or work

Going places together

EXAMPLE G
A good friend:

Cares about me

Spends time with me

Is someone I can talk to about my problems

Is someone I can have fun with

SECTION 5
SEXUAL AWARENESS

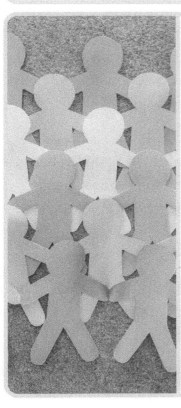

- Building a Positive Self-Image

- Identifying Gender

- Identifying Body Parts and Understanding Their Functions

- Understanding Public and Private Behavior

- Differentiating Between Inappropriate and Appropriate Touching

- Understanding the Emotional and Physical Changes of Puberty

- Understanding Sexual Feelings and Behaviors

- Understanding Reproduction

- Examining Societal Norms and Values Regarding Sexual Behavior

- Learning about Sexually Transmitted Infections

"I strongly believed that Pam was a victim, not because of her intellectual disability, but because she did not know anything about sex."
— A counselor at a rape crisis center

SEXUAL AWARENESS

Along with being social, we are sexual beings. From an early age, most of us began to discover our sexuality. As children, we wondered: "Where do babies come from? Why don't girls have a penis? Will I get breasts when I grow up?" How the people in our lives responded to the curiosity and provided information shaped our attitudes and behaviors about sexuality.

For most people, the desire for sexual knowledge and identity continues into adulthood as concerns naturally broaden to include issues of intimacy, fertility, sexual dysfunction, sexually transmitted infections, and personal and societal values related to sexual expression. This includes people with developmental disabilities who may or may not actively seek information or ask questions about sexuality. In the past, support providers were often misguided and used excuses to avoid the topic of sex. "We think they won't understand. If they do, we are afraid what they will do with the knowledge." "We think their parents will get upset." "We are embarrassed to talk about it." or "We don't know how to talk about sexuality." As a result, many adults with developmental disabilities lack basic sexual knowledge, are easily manipulated by others, and lack guidelines for the expression of sexual feelings.

Some of the young adults with whom we have worked have been taught to avoid sex because it is bad is and something they shouldn't talk about and certainly should not engage in. Other young people we have encountered have been given no direction regarding sexual expression. Their unacceptable behaviors have been excused by caregivers because of a belief that the person is incapable of learning otherwise or controlling himself/herself/themselves.

Through our experiences, we have come to strongly believe that all individuals benefit from accurate information about human sexuality. Knowledge about the body and how it works heightens self-confidence, increases self-esteem, and allays misconceptions and fears.

Fundamental to human sexuality is our experience of biologic sex and gender identity. In conversation, these words are often used interchangeably, but understanding their differing definitions can be helpful. Sex refers to a person's anatomy, such as their genitalia, or other characteristics, such as breasts or body hair. We are all generally assigned a sex at birth; for example, babies born with a penis are assigned a sex of male. Gender refers to our internal concept of who we are: male, female, a blend of both, or something else. For instance, someone who has a gender identity that is different than their sex assigned at birth is transgender.

In addition to sex and gender identity, sexual orientation is also fundamentally important. Sexual orientation refers to the gender of persons to which someone has enduring emotional, romantic, or sexual attraction. It exists on a spectrum that can change over time, from being exclusively attracted to men to being exclusively attracted to women, with a wide range in the middle. Also, some people may experience little or no sexual attraction to anyone and identify as asexual.

SECTION 5: SEXUAL AWARENESS

Like anyone else, people with developmental disabilities may have confusing feelings about their own gender identity, sexual orientation, or both. They may not understand why they feel different than most of their friends and classmates. Or they may meet a gay couple or transgender person and not understand what that means. As part of teaching people with developmental disabilities about human sexuality, we believe it is also critical to teach about gender identity and sexual orientation.

Just as some participants may experience discomfort in talking about explicit aspects of sex, some support people may also experience discomfort. This usually subsides with practice and experience. When we answer questions, discuss issues, and give support and guidance, people with developmental disabilities are more likely to exercise self-control, master concepts, and make informed choices. If people with developmental disabilities develop an understanding of sexual feelings, there is a greater likelihood that sexuality will be expressed in acceptable and responsible ways, and that risks of sexual abuse will be lessened.

GOAL 1: Building a Positive Self-Image

Activities:

1. Review activities under Goal #1: Building a Positive Self-Image, in Understanding Relationships, page 25.

   Positive Self-Image

2. Ask each participant to (a) tell something that they like about how they look and (b) tell something that they would like to change, if they could. Compare ourselves with others and accept our differences. Help participants identify eye color, facial characteristics, hair color and texture, and body type (for example, tall or short) among the group. Note that everyone is different and each person is "okay." Perhaps someone in the group uses a wheelchair, has difficulty speaking, or is visually impaired—these are other examples of differences.

   Accepting Differences

Maintaining Personal Appearance

3. Discuss ways that we take care of ourselves and keep ourselves looking good.

   ➤ Include washing/bathing, eating healthy foods, brushing teeth, getting enough sleep, brushing or combing hair and exercise/activity.

   ➤ List other things that people do to keep themselves looking good, such as wearing makeup, wearing jewelry, going to the hair salon/barber shop, wearing braces on teeth, and getting a manicure.

GOAL 2: Identifying Gender

Activities:

Gender Identification

1. Help participants develop a basic understanding of gender identification. Have them cut out pictures from magazines of people, and paste them on a piece of paper. Discuss typical female and male characteristics. Look at the pictures and discuss gender differences. Use this activity to dispel stereotypes and discuss uniqueness of individuals.

2. Have participants share their gender identity. Be prepared to acknowledge in a sensitive and nonjudgmental way if a youth presents him- or herself as gender variant or shares awareness about someone else who is gender variant. For example, a youth may identify as transgender, which is an adjective describing an individual whose gender identity and sex assigned at birth are different. For instance, an individual's assigned sex may be male, but the gender identity may be female. Some individuals may also identify as having a blend of male and female or no gender.

Gender Roles and Stereotypes

3. Help participants explore roles and behavior of men and women in today's society. Use books and pictures to identify males and females in a variety of non-stereotyped roles. Dispel stereotypes such as "men don't cry", or "only women take care of babies," or "men are doctors, women are teachers and nurses."

4. Discuss sexual orientation. For more information, refer to Goal #7: Understanding Sexual Feelings and Behaviors, Activity #3, page 50.

GOAL 3: Identifying Body Parts and Understanding Their Functions

It is important that people with disabilities feel as comfortable with identifying and labeling their sexual body parts as they do with any other body part. Knowing about one's whole body is important for self-concept. It is also important to have understandable words to be able to communicate to others about one's sexual parts. This includes using words to tell someone about being in pain or injured, about an experience of sexual abusive behavior, or to tell a partner what is pleasurable to the person.

When teaching about body parts, it is best to use pictures or drawings that are clear and simple (see illustrations in the Sexual Attitudes and Knowledge Assessment in Section Seven for examples). Show internal organs as they appear in the whole body, so the participants can visualize the location of the body part. Showing a body part separate from the body may be confusing. See the Appendix for the glossary that contains a listing of descriptions of body parts.

Activities

1. Review the location and function of non-sexual body parts using pictures, drawings, or anatomically correct dolls. Have the participants identify body parts in one or both of two ways: (1) point to the part and ask the person to name it, and/or (2) name the part and ask the person to point to it. Talk about the function of the body parts—for example, "What are arms used for?" "What are ears used for?" "What is the stomach for?" and so forth.

Identifying Body Parts and Understanding Their Function

> Review external body parts (the parts of the body that we can see). Use the basic body parts (arms, legs, eyes, hair, and so forth) and don't become too detailed (avoid parts such as phalanges or palpebral fissures.)

> Review internal body parts (those parts inside our bodies that we cannot see). Include only the basic body parts, such as stomach, muscles, heart, and blood.

Identifying Sexual Body Parts and Understanding Their Functions

2. Draw an outline of a man or woman on a large sheet of paper, leaving out all the details. What parts would they add for the picture for it to be a typical man? To be a typical woman? Have group members draw in the parts, adding as many details as they can, including genitals and body hair. Review the location and function of sexual body parts. *Note*: For this and the following activities, be prepared to recognize, in a sensitive and non-judgmental way, that some people may have variant sexual anatomy and/or changed gender. For more information, refer to Goal #2: Identifying Gender, Activity #2, page 56.

Female Body Parts

3. Female body parts.
   > Using the female adult drawing in the Appendix, have the group members identify the sexual parts for the female in the following ways: (a) pointing to the part after the group leader names it, or (b) naming the part after the group leader points to it. Identify breast area, pubic area, and vulva. Talk about internal parts, including the uterus, ovary, and egg (ovum.) Also discuss urinary opening, anus, and vagina, which are the three openings in the woman's "bottom" or "crotch" area. These openings and the buttocks are other areas that are considered private areas (For activities on private/public, see Goal #4: Understanding Public and Private Behavior, page 60.

   > In simple, understandable terms, explain the function of the female sexual parts. For example, you might say that the female has two ovaries, one on each side low in the abdomen (or belly). The ovaries store the female sex cells called "eggs" or "ova." Be careful to clarify that these eggs are not the size of chicken eggs that we cook and eat, but that they are very tiny,

SECTION 5: SEXUAL AWARENESS

the size of a pin head. Have the youth tell you their understanding of the function of the sexual parts. (To include this with the discussion of intercourse and conception, refer to Goal #7: Understanding Sexual Feelings and Behaviors, page 68 and Goal #8: Understanding Reproduction, page 71.) Group members can also locate and describe the function of other female body parts like clitoris, fallopian tubes, and ovaries.

4. Male body parts.

> Using a drawing of an adult male (see Assessment in Section Seven for illustration) have group members identify the sexual parts for male in the following ways, (1) pointing to the part after the group leader names it, or (2) naming the part after the group leader points to it. At a minimum include the penis, testicles, anus, and pubic area.

Male Body Parts

> In simple understandable words, explain the function of the male sexual parts. For example: Sperm is the male sex cell, so tiny one can't see it without a microscope, and it is produced by the testicles.

> Have the students tell you the function of the sexual part you have discussed to check their understanding. (See Sexual Awareness, Goal #7: Understanding Sexual Feelings and Behaviors and Goal #8: Understanding Reproduction, to include this with the discussion of intercourse and conception.) Other specific male body sexual parts may also be discussed with group members who may be able to understand more detail, including parts of the penis (glans and shaft), scrotum, sperm ducts, and so on.

5. Have group members list the slang words for each sexual part. Explain that slang words are "made-up" words. Some people get upset when they hear those words or they don't understand what the term means. It is best to use the correct word, the "dictionary word" for the sexual part.

Slang Words

6. Discuss that everyone's body looks different from others, including their sexual parts. Just as hair and eye color differ, so do body height and weight and the size and shape of sexual body parts. For example, talk about the fact that some women have small breasts and some women have large

Accepting Differences

breasts; some men have a small penis and some men have a large penis. Even though we are all different, we are still "okay."

GOAL 4: Understanding Public and Private Behavior

Activities:

Private and Privacy

1. Review the concepts of privacy and private.

   > Privacy is when no one else is around.

   > We all have the right to be alone (to be private) at times. We need to respect others' need for privacy.

   > Your body has private parts.

   > Some activities are private and need to be done in private places, such as using the toilet, usually when no one else is around.

   > Sexuality is a private matter; talk about it only with certain people.

   > Social media is not a private place.

Private Places

2. Help group members identify their "private" places, including at home (bedroom, bathroom) or at school or work (locker, desk, bathroom). Talk about the importance of each person respecting the privacy of others. For example, participants may want to have a PRIVATE sign to use on a bedroom door.

Private Body Parts

3. Discuss what parts of the body are considered "private." Talk about sexual and other related parts, including genital areas, breasts and buttocks. Using drawings of a male and female (see Section Seven for examples of illustrations), have participants identify the private parts of the body by drawing or pasting a picture of a bathing suit or underwear. Anatomically correct dolls are useful for demonstrating this concept.

SECTION 5: SEXUAL AWARENESS

4. Discuss "private" activities and behavior—things that we do in private places, when other people are not around. Identify activities that are done in private places, including bathing, taking a shower, using the toilet, undressing/dressing, touching your own sexual parts for pleasure (masturbation), and sexual behavior (for example, kissing, sexual touching and intercourse.) *Note*: This is a good time to stress the importance of not posting or sharing pictures of anyone's private parts on social media.

   Private Activities

5. Introduce the concept of "public," that is, when other people are around.

   Public

6. Help group members identify "public" places, including at home (kitchen, living room, or yard), at school or work (office, classroom), or in the community (store, bus stop.) Combine with, Goal #4: Understanding Public and Private Behavior, Activity #2, page 60, above.

   Public Places

7. Discuss what parts of the body are considered "public." *Note*: This may vary according to cultural beliefs or family background. Use drawings of a male and female (see Section Seven: Assessments for illustrations) to point out the "public" parts—or the parts of the body that are "okay" for other people to see. Anatomically correct dolls are also useful for demonstrating this concept. Combine with Goal #4: Understanding Public and Private Behavior, Activity #3 above (private body parts), page 60. Remind group members that even if a part is a public part, that "you don't have to be touched anywhere on your body if you don't want to. See Goal #5: Differentiating Between inappropriate and Appropriate Touch, page 62.

   Public Body Parts

8. Discuss "public" activities or behavior. These include those things that are "ok" to do in front of other people. Combine this discussion with Goal #4: Understanding Public and Private Behavior Activity #7 (public body parts), page 61.

   Public Activities

9. Discuss when, where, and with whom it is okay to talk about sexuality. Some people need explicit guidelines to follow. Include safeguards related to social media. See Appendix: Resources for references on Cyber Safety.

10. Address individual needs of group members regarding private/public activities and behaviors.

> You may need to discuss the fact that some participants need help with bathing and toileting. This might require the caregiver to touch private parts in order to assist toileting or bathing, activities that are considered private, occurring in a private place. Discuss with the participant individually as needed.

> For some participants to learn socially acceptable behavior, it may be necessary to give individualized instruction with specific rules about "private" and "public" behavior and places. For example, it may be "okay" to touch themselves, or masturbate, in the shower or the bathroom in their home (which are "private" places), but it would not be "okay" to masturbate in the bathroom or shower while at school or work (these are more like "public" places.)

> As a support provider, think about how you respond to a person if the person engages in a "private" activity (for example, masturbation) in a non-private or public place. It is usually best to interrupt the behavior and give information about if, when, and where the behavior is "okay." Then redirect to another activity. Avoid scolding and instead use a supportive, teaching approach.

GOAL 5: Differentiating Between Inappropriate and Appropriate Touching

Activities:

Private and
Public Body
Parts

1. Review the concepts of private and public body parts. Which parts can be shown in public? Which parts are covered in public? For specific activities, refer above to Goal #4: Understanding Public and Private Behavior, Activities #3 and #7, page 61. Recognize cultural differences in private and

public body parts. For example, some Muslim women cover their heads in public.

2. Review private and public behavior and activities. For specific activities, refer to Goal #4: Understanding Public and Private Behavior, Activities #4 and #8, page 61.

Private and Public Activities

3. Talk about rules for touching of private parts.

> Review with group members that in most cases, no one should touch another person unless he/she/they want to be touched on either public or private parts.

> Discuss that there are certain times when it is okay for certain people to touch private parts. For example, a parent, nurse, physician, or other caregiver may need to touch a private part to examine you or if you are sick or hurt. Or if you are mature enough to be sexual with another person, and both of you agree that touching of private parts is okay.

4. Help group members identify types of touches. Talk about:

Types of "Touches"

> "Good" touches—a nurturing touch that feels like something is being given or shared, such as a hug, holding hands with a friend or a family member, having your sister brush your hair, and a back rub. Think about how nice these things feel.

> "Bad" touches—a touch that is painful or feels like something is being taken away, like when someone hits or kicks you, a mosquito biting or a bee stinging you, or bruising your knee when you fall down. Think about how bad or "yucky" these things feel. A "bad" touch might also be when someone touches you in a private place (as in sexual abuse) or in a way that feels bad or that you don't want.

> "Confusing" touch—any touch that cannot be clearly labeled as bad or good. Any touch may become "confusing" when (1) the meaning of the touch is not clear, (2) the person doing the touching doesn't usually behave in this way, or (3) the touching becomes sexual and the receiver is

confused about it. For example, sometimes things in the "good" touch list don't feel good—like getting hugged by a relative when you don't want to be hugged. Another example is when someone you like and who is usually nice to you touches you in a way that feels uncomfortable—for example, tickling too long or touching you in a private place.

5. Address inappropriate touching. Use examples of different situations to help individuals figure out inappropriate touching by combining aspects of public and private and socially appropriate behavior. For example, "Is it okay to touch your brother's penis?" "Is it okay to touch you own penis or vulva when you are in a public place?"

> Refer to Section Six: Assertiveness for activities for learning how to avoid or respond to unwanted touches.

GOAL 6: Understanding the Emotional and Physical Changes of Puberty

This original STARS guidebook is designed for older adolescents and adults. Many of these individuals for whom this book is intended will have gone through puberty already. However, a review of the changes during puberty may be helpful for group members who would like a review or who have not learned about their bodies and puberty.

Activities:

Understanding Developmental Stages

1. Ask participants to bring photographs of themselves at different ages. Discuss how their bodies have changed from birth. If photographs aren't available, cut pictures out of magazines of people at different stages of development.

Understanding Puberty

2. Explain puberty using simple terms and understandable ideas. For example, you might include that at a certain point or time period in your life, usually when you were around ten or eleven years old, your body knew that

it was time to change to become an adult. This time is called puberty, and your body began to change to look more like an adult. Changes take place both inside and outside the body. Some are obvious, and others occur inside the body that we cannot see. Have group members tell you about puberty to review their understanding.

3. Review specific body changes that happened during puberty. Identify specific characteristics that make grown-ups look different from children—height, body hair, breasts, and big muscles. Use pictures to demonstrate these differences.

> **Body Changes During Puberty**

> In girls, the changes that appear in puberty include: Breasts start to enlarge, pubic hair appears, hair appears under the arms, body grows taller, and menstruation begins.

> In boys, the changes that appear in puberty include: Testes and penis get bigger, pubic hair appears, voice changes, ejaculation becomes possible, body grows taller, hair appears under arms and on legs and chest, and beard develops.

4. Explain that during puberty, girls begin to experience an increase in sexual feelings in addition to body changes, which gradually lessen as the female grows older. Having sexy dreams and fantasies and becoming sexually excited is a normal part of growing up. Emphasize in the discussion that just because a young woman has become aware of sexual feelings or sexual arousal does not mean it is necessary to act on them with others (be explicit about explaining intimate behavior with others).

Changes in Females

5. Explain menstruation or period. Use simple and understandable words. There is a wide spectrum of needs for information among women with cognitive limitations, and it is important to consider what amount is needed for each woman. Consider whether the woman needs just enough information to understand that menstruation is normal for adult women, and whether more information would be too abstract and confusing for her. Or consider whether the woman needs much more information because she

Menstruation

has higher cognitive capabilities and she is capable of understanding that a female can become pregnant after she has begun menstruating.

> Explain that menstruation happens to typical females only. It begins during puberty when a girl's body is developing, and she is becoming a woman. It is a natural process that will happen until a woman is in her forties or fifties. It is also called a period.

> Use pictures or an anatomically correct doll to show as explicitly as possible where the menstrual blood flows. Ask the group members to tell you about menstruation to check their understanding, including slang words.

> Point out to those women who will understand that when a girl is mature enough to menstruate, her body has gone through changes that make it possible for her to become pregnant. (See Goal #7: Understanding Sexual Feelings and Behaviors, page 68, below for activities regarding intercourse and pregnancy.)

> Review use of feminine hygiene products. Women may appreciate the opportunity to view the products without men present. Find out if any group members need specific training about menstrual management, and arrange to provide that training yourself or by asking a significant other to assist with the training.

> Young men will also benefit from basic information about menstruation. It can help them to better understand the female body and what girls are going through, and to clarify any misinformation. Provide the opportunity to young men to view feminine hygiene products and give a brief explanation. Some of the more explicit discussion and use of feminine hygiene products by women may be best done with women only.

> Discuss other concerns about menstruation including cramps, recording menstrual cycles, managing pre-menstrual syndrome (PMS), and minor uncomfortable symptoms. Identify supportive strategies for managing symptoms.

6. Address menopause. Explain what happens to a woman's body during menopause. Some individuals may need support if they are going through menopause. It is important that caregivers understand the impact and possible changes for the woman, as well as strategies for managing symptoms.

Menopause

7. Explain the changes that boys experience during puberty. Most young men will experience a normal increase in sexual feelings, causing more frequent erections of their penis, which is normal. Having sexy dreams and fantasies and becoming sexually excited is a normal part of growing up. Emphasize, though, that it is not necessary to act on sexual feelings (be explicit about intimate behavior with others) just because the youth becomes aware of these feelings.

Changes in Males

8. Explain an erection using simple understandable terms. Figure out how much detail to use based on the understanding capabilities of the men. Show tasteful (not pornographic) pictures of males to compare the penis in a flaccid state and in an erect state.

Erection

> In a basic discussion, you might say that an erection is when the penis gets stiff and hard when a boy or man is sexually excited. It can happen often when a boy is going through puberty, sometimes from seeing a sexually attractive person or from physical stimulation from clothing or touching. It happens less often as males mature. Remind the men that if an erection happens when they are in a public place, it is not "okay" to touch their penis. Sometimes ejaculation occurs with an erection. (See Goal #6: Understanding the Physical and Emotional Changes of Puberty, Activity #9, page 68, below, for an explanation of ejaculation.)

> Females also benefit from basic information about male functions. It will help them to better understand the male body and what men experience and to clarify any misinformation. If presenting information in a group setting, the decision to share this information with a mixed gender group, or with specific genders separately, depends on the comfort level of the adult facilitator and individual participants.

> Discuss erection in more detail, linking erection with intercourse, for men who will understand. To explain, you might say that males are built the way they are and have erections of their penis because that is part of the process of creating babies. A male's penis is designed to be able to fit inside a woman's vagina, and it needs to be erect to do that. Emphasize that most erections, while a sign of sexual excitement, do not result in intercourse or reproduction.

> Identify the slang words for erection paired with the word erection.

> It may come up in discussion that some men use medications to enhance erections. Suggest that their health care provider would be a good source of information regarding specific products and their uses.

Ejaculation

9. Explain ejaculation. Use simple, understandable terms. To explain, you might say that when older boys and men are sexually excited, the penis has an erection. If the penis is stimulated enough, the male will have an orgasm, which is a very strong and good feeling in the area around the penis. At the time of the orgasm, a thick, white fluid called semen, which carries sperm, comes out quickly from the end of the penis (about a tablespoonful). Check the understanding of the men by asking them to explain ejaculation.

> Identify slang words for ejaculation.

GOAL 7: Understanding Sexual Feelings and Behaviors

Activities:

1. Review concepts of romantic relationships. For specific activities, see Goal #4: Engaging in More Mature Relationships, in Section Four: Social Interaction, page 43.

SECTION 5: SEXUAL AWARENESS

2. Discuss behaviors that are considered sexual, as well as the range of sexual behaviors that can be associated with a romantic relationship. It is also important to consider cultural and family values along with social rules that are related to sexual expression. For specific activities, see Goal #9: Examining Societal Norms and Values Regarding Sexuality, page 75.

   ➤ List behaviors that two people in a romantic relationship might do to express their affection for each other, such as giving compliments and gifts, holding hands, hugging, kissing sexual touching, and intercourse. Discuss current terms/words for sexual touching. Help group members understand which behaviors are acceptable in a romantic relationship but not acceptable in non-romantic relationships.

3. Discuss sexual orientation. This refers to the gender or genders to which a person has sexual, emotional, or romantic attraction. Some people have or want a sexual partner of the opposite gender to care about and to have sexual relations with—this sexual orientation is called heterosexual. Other people have or want a sexual partner of the same gender to care about and have a sexual relationship with—this is referred to as gay or lesbian sexual orientation. For more discussion activities, see Goal #9: Examining Society Norms and Values Regarding Sexuality, page 75.

4. Discuss masturbation. You might say that masturbation is when a person of any gender identity touches their own sexual parts (private parts or genitals) by stroking or rubbing them, which feels very good and sexually stimulating. Use an illustration (see S.A.K. Assessment in Section Seven for examples of pictures). Emphasize that masturbation is done in a private place and identify these possible places with the group members. See Goal #4: Understanding Public and Private Behavior, Activity #4, page 60 above, to combine this with a discussion of private and public behavior. Also refer to Goal #9: Examining Societal Norms and Values Regarding Sexuality, Activity #1, page 75 above, to combine this discussion with values about sexual behavior.

Sexual Expression

Sexual Orientation

Masturbation

Orgasm

5. Explain orgasm. Orgasm can happen in all people Explain that when a person of any gender identity is sexually excited, he/she/they may experience a build-up of sexual (erotic) tension. The heart usually beats faster and stronger, and there is more rapid breathing and increased muscular tension. This tension increases to a certain level until there is a release, which is often somewhat sudden. After the release, there is usually a feeling of pleasure, relaxation, or relief. In typical females, orgasm usually involves the clitoris and surrounding area. In typical males, orgasm involves the penis, scrotum, and surrounding pelvis area. Orgasm can happen as a result of masturbation or intercourse. In men, ejaculation is not the same as orgasm, but these two actions usually happen together. For more discussion on erection and ejaculation, see Goal #6: Understanding the Emotional and Physical Changes of Puberty, page 64.

Intercourse

6. Explain intercourse. First review male and female sexual body parts, including penis, vulva/vagina, and erection. Your explanation needs to be simple and understandable. You might say that "when a grown man and a grown woman love each other in a sexual way, they may want to have intercourse. While they are in a private place they usually get sexually excited by kissing, hugging, and touching each other on their bodies, including their private parts. When a man gets sexually excited, this penis will become erect, and when a woman gets excited, her vagina/vulva may become moist from secretions. Intercourse is when the man puts his erect penis into the woman's vagina. Moving back and forth can feel very good, and usually orgasms occur for both the woman and the man (he will usually ejaculate sperm). This is the way a woman can become pregnant."

   ➤ This discussion may be combined with content on the prevention of pregnancy, both abstinence and contraception. For activities, see Goal #8: Understanding Reproduction in Section Five: Sexual Awareness. Emphasize the benefits of a monogamous relationship.

Virgin

7. Discuss what it means to be a virgin. This is a word used to describe a person who has not had sexual intercourse. Reinforce that it is okay for a person to be a virgin and for some people it is a healthy choice.

SECTION 5: SEXUAL AWARENESS

GOAL 8: Understanding Reproduction

Activities:

1. Explain fertilization. Review internal and external sexual body parts, which is discussed in Goal #3: Identifying Body Parts and Understanding Their Functions, page 57, and intercourse, which is discussed in Goal #7: Understanding Sexual Feelings and Behaviors, Activity #6, page 70.

   > Explain by saying that fertilization happens during or after intercourse. If it is the time of the month when a woman's ovary has produced an egg (an ovum), the act of intercourse could result in fertilization and a pregnancy. This occurs when sperm meets up with the egg in the woman's body and the egg is fertilized and attaches to the uterine wall.

   > In your discussion, be clear about the size of the egg—that it is very tiny, not like a chicken egg. Do not use terminology like "planting a seed," as some books would suggest. People with cognitive disabilities usually think very concretely, and they could take this very literally, meaning that they "plant a seed, an apple seed or a watermelon seed" in their vagina if they want to have a baby.

   > Help participants understand that pregnancy is a result of intercourse, and check for understanding.

   Fertilization

2. Discuss pregnancy. In most cases, pregnancy happens only after a man and a woman have had intercourse, and fertilization occurs when the egg in the woman meets with the sperm from the man. The fertilized ovum, which attaches to the uterine wall, starts growing there. Pregnancy normally lasts nine months. After about four months, the mother's abdomen begins to get noticeably larger as the baby grows inside the uterus. Clarify that the baby does not grow in the stomach (where our food goes), but in the uterus. Check group members' understanding by having them describe pregnancy, using pictures or anatomically correct dolls.

   Pregnancy

> Be prepared to acknowledge that individuals may share knowledge or experiences about other means of fertilization and pregnancy. For example to have a child, two male partners may use a surrogate, or two female partners may use a sperm donor.

> Discuss the concepts of twins and other multiple births.

> Other areas for discussion, especially for those individuals who have the capability to understand, might include how a woman knows she is pregnant. Talk about having intercourse, missing a period, noticing some physical changes, and going to the doctor for a pregnancy test and then prenatal care.

Labor and Delivery

3. Explain labor and the birthing process to help group members understand how the baby gets out of the mother's body. A birth of a baby usually occurs in the hospital where doctors and nurses can help. Talk about both types of births, vaginal delivery, and Cesarean section (C-section). Pictures or anatomical models that show the whole woman's body during delivery are helpful. (Sometimes, these can be borrowed from public schools or agencies that sponsor birthing classes). Explain that labor and birth are a lot of work for the woman, and although painful, most woman say that birthing a baby is worth it.

> Explain the umbilical cord and the umbilicus, or belly button. The baby and mother are connected inside by the umbilical cord of the baby and the inside of the mother's uterus with the placenta, so that the baby gets enough nourishment and oxygen in the uterus. Once the baby is outside the mother's body, this umbilical cord isn't needed anymore and is cut off. The resulting belly button is where this cord was located.

> Sometimes a video of the birthing process is useful for those who are capable of understanding this content. Think carefully, though, about whether this is helpful for individuals to see and for whom. Always be sure to preview the video before showing and be certain to prepare individuals for what they will see.

SECTION 5: SEXUAL AWARENESS

4. Discuss prevention of pregnancy by abstaining from intercourse. This is the only sure way to prevent pregnancy. Assure group members that sexual feelings are normal when in an intimate relationship, but sexual intercourse is not the only way to express those feelings. To achieve successful abstinence from intercourse, it is helpful to identify ways to avoid situations in which intercourse can easily happen. For example, you might choose social activities in a group instead of only with your intimate partner, recognizing that it may be hard to stop from having sexual activity if you and your partner are in a private place and get sexually excited. Remind group members that each person can make their own decision about engaging in sexual intercourse and do not need to be concerned with only pleasing their partner or giving in to peer pressure.

Abstinence

5. Discuss the prevention of pregnancy by using contraception, or birth control. To promote understanding for group members, a discussion of contraception should follow a review of intercourse and the process of fertilization. (For specific activities, see Goal #7: Understanding Sexual Feelings and Behaviors, Activity #6, page 70 , and Goal #8: Understanding Reproduction, Activity #1, page 71 above.)

Birth Control/ Contraception

> ➤ You might explain that when a man and woman are very much in love and want to show their love through intercourse, but they do not want to have a baby, they can prevent pregnancy through birth control or contraception. Birth control stops the sperm and egg from coming together to produce a fertilized egg, which grows into a baby.

> ➤ Assess each participant's need for information about birth control. Not all group members need to have detailed information. Generally, if a person can understand intercourse, then the person can likely understand the concept of birth control. The most essential information to provide about birth control includes (1) why it is used, (2) when to use it, (3) different types of methods, and (4) who can help the person to obtain birth control.

> Be cautious about presenting many specific types of birth control measures at one time, as this may be confusing for the person, especially for a person with an intellectual disability. Instead, arrange for a one-to-one conversation with the person to provide direction about the best type of birth control for his/her abilities and situation.

> Assist group members in identifying helpful adults to discuss birth control—perhaps a physician, nurse practitioner, or family planning clinic in the community would be places to go. Talk about how to ask for information and support about birth control.

> Provide specific instruction of birth control methods as indicated. For example, providing information about using condoms is helpful for many reasons. Condoms are used to prevent pregnancy and the transmission of sexually transmitted infections. Condoms are readily available in stores and many people have heard of them.

> If information about condom use is shared, individuals with intellectual disabilities will need explicit information about condoms, that is, knowing exactly when and how to use a condom. Do not make anyone uncomfortable by demonstrating use of a condom on a human, but instead demonstrate its use on a life-sized model of a penis. Be sure to explain step-by-step specifics of condom use: once the penis is erect, and before intercourse, put the condom on by placing it on the tip of the penis and gently unrolling it down toward the body, and so on. Other essential information to include: latex condoms are safest; condoms in wrappers are safe for six months, and after that, discard to avoid chance of breaking or tearing; condoms are best with non-oxynyl9, a jelly-like substance that coats the condom and acts as a spermicide (to prevent pregnancy).

Sterilization

6. Explain sterilization. This means methods of birth control that are permanent. Sterilization is suitable only for those men and women who are able to give consent and who have decided never to cause conception or become pregnant. There are laws about who can be sterilized.

7. Explain abortion. Explain that abortion is a surgical procedure done by a licensed physician (i.e. medical doctor) to end a pregnancy before the time when the baby would be grown enough to be born, usually sometime within the first one to four months of pregnancy. In addition, a licensed medical doctor can prescribe a dose of certain medications for the purposes of abortion. Emphasize that an abortion is a serious procedure to remove the fetus and placenta and that is performed by a doctor in a medical clinic or hospital. You must never attempt to perform an abortion yourself. Abortion should not be substituted for the use of other birth control measures. Abortion is legal in the United States, but people have differing views on whether abortion is ethical or moral, and the availability of abortion varies greatly among states in the US.

Abortion

GOAL 9: Examining Societal Norms and Values Regarding Sexuality

Note: For this section, it is important to acknowledge possible variations among cultural and family beliefs that may affect acceptable sexual behavior.

Activities:

1. In a group or individual discussion, explore beliefs about the rules of society that govern sexual behavior. Present the concept of values and social rules as guidelines that we go by to know how to act in an acceptable way. For example, what rules are there in your home or in your workplace? Each type of setting where group members live, work, and recreate will have its own rules and expectations regarding sexual activity. Individuals in the group may be living in a variety of residential settings. These settings could include their family home, a group home, or a supported apartment. Group members may be working or spending their days in a variety of vocational, educational, or recreational settings as well. List values or social rules for

Influence of Social Rules and Personal Values on Sexual Behavior

each of the sexual activities (i.e., when the behaviors are okay and when they are not). For example, discuss:

➤ When it is okay to hug someone?

➤ How well should you know someone before you touch each other in a sexual way?

➤ When is it okay to have intimate sexual relations? You might start the discussion with, "Some people have strong feelings about sexual relations and that it is only okay if the couple is married. Other people have different values/ideas and feel that if two people care about each other very much and they want to express their love with sexual relations, it is okay even if they are not married. What do you think?"

➤ Masturbation is a healthy and normal activity, but it is also a value-laden behavior. Check in with participants: What have you learned about masturbation? What have people told you? Is it okay? When and where is it okay to do? Emphasize that it needs to be done in a private place. Inquire whether participants have a private place if they wish to engage in masturbation.

➤ Sexual Orientation. Our society is moving towards greater acceptance of individuals with differing sexual orientations. However, some people, cultures, and religions are not accepting of same-sex relationships and they have differing ideas about relationships. Remind participants that there are slang terms which are rude and hurtful, including "fag," "dyke," or "homo," and that should never be used. Give examples of terms/words that are currently acceptable and respectful when referring to sexual orientation.

Mutual Consent

2. Present the concept of mutual consent in sexual behavior. consent means that people engaging in the sexual behavior agree that it is wanted, whether it is touching, hugging, kissing, or intercourse. Otherwise, if someone does not want to engage in the behavior, then the consent isn't mutual. If

issues related to sexual assault are raised in course of the discussion, refer to Section Six: Assertiveness for specific activities.

3. Address decision-making about engaging in sexual situations. This discussion makes the most sense when an individual is dating or thinking about a romantic relationship. Discuss some important things to think about when making decisions about showing sexual feelings. This section may be useful in helping participants who are in serious romantic relationships to consider their options and their behavior. Help them consider:

Personal Decision-Making

> Ask the person: Do you feel like you're ready, and do you feel like you can be responsible for your actions, which affect you and another person?

> Advise the person: Be sure the other person feels just as you do. Never force anyone into anything.

> Guide the person to a supportive adult: If you can, discuss these issues with An adult you trust, perhaps your parent, guardian, support worker, or friend. Who is a safe and supportive adult for you?

> Advise the person: Think about sexual behavior ahead of time, that is, before being in a situation that necessitates decision-making.

> Discuss how a person might know that he/she is ready for a sexual relationship. To be ready to engage in sexual behavior, it is best if a person has the ability to:

❑ Understand that the enjoyment of this aspect of sexuality involves the ability to make thoughtful decisions.

❑ Talk comfortably, either verbally or with augmentative communication, with their partner about taking precautions for preventing pregnancy or sexually transmitted infections (STIs.) Is the person capable of sharing the responsibility for carrying out these precautions?

❑ Understand whether they are exploiting another person or being exploited.

❑ Make the emotional commitment and take on the obligation of a healthy adult sexual relationship.

4. Use a story to discuss decision-making. Sometimes it is easier for group members to use a story about someone else when thinking about sensitive situations related to sexuality. Use pictures in books or magazines and develop a story for the participants to relate to. Develop stories to illustrate some of the relationship issues that group members may be experiencing. For example, the following story makes the point that there are other ways to express feelings and to be with your intimate sexual partner than just to have sex.

"Suppose that Kim and Eric care about each other very much and have very strong emotional feelings for each other. They both have decided they are not ready for sexual intercourse, but they do want to share their sexual feelings. What are ways they can show their affection? How can they figure out what they will do?" Answers may include: talk to each other, talk to a trusted adult to help give suggestions.

To review sexual behaviors in romantic relationships, refer to Goal #7: Understanding Sexual Feelings and Behaviors, page 68.

Present other brief situations and ask group members for their opinions about what they would do. You can list two to three alternatives for each situation, and then discuss what might be the consequences of that decision.

GOAL 10: Learning about Sexually Transmitted Infections

Activities:

1. To help group members grasp the concept of sexually transmitted infections, it is helpful to talk about how other common infections are spread.

Review how people get common infections; most are spread from person to person. For example, the common cold is spread from germs that are passed by sneezing into the air, which is breathed in by another person, or sneezing onto the hands and then touching another person. Another example is that a person can get poison ivy by touching the leaves of a poison ivy plant to the skin.

Understanding Sexually Transmitted Infections

2. "STIs" or sexually transmitted infections (formerly called sexually transmitted diseases) are infections which can be spread by germs through having sexual contact with someone who has the infection. Clarify that the only way to "catch" a STI is through sexual contact with someone who already has the infection. Be explicit about describing the sexual contact: for example, vagina and penis; vagina and mouth; penis and anus. Anatomically correct dolls are useful for this.

3. Review some of the names of the infections, identifying both the slang words and the medical terminology: gonorrhea, herpes, chlamydia, syphilis, AIDS.

Types of STIs

4. Other important points about STIs:

   ➤ If you have not had sexual contact, you don't need to worry about having caught a STI.

   ➤ If you are considering having sexual contact with a partner, it is essential to know how to prevent the spread of STIs. Emphasize the importance of being able to talk with your sexual partner about STIs. This means that you know them well enough so that you can discuss sexual habits and determine whether you can trust them to be honest about the following:

   ❑ Ask your partner if he/she/they might have an infection of the sexual parts.

   ❑ Use "safer sex" practices, such as using a condom or having no sexual contact.

> If you find out your sex partner has a sexually transmitted infection and you have had sexual contact, you should be checked by a health care provider, even if you don't have symptoms.

Symptoms of STI's

5. Review the symptoms that may indicate that a person has a sexually transmitted Infection. If these symptoms are present, then the person needs to be checked by a health care provider. The symptoms may include discharge from the penis or vagina that is difference than usual and sores, rashes, itching, blisters, or pain around the genitals. Sometimes these symptoms are due to an STI, and sometimes they result from causes other than an STI, such as a urinary tract infection.

HIV/AIDS

6. You may want to discuss human immunodeficiency virus (HIV) infection. Points to include:

> The serious nature of the HIV infection, the course of the infection to AIDS, and treatment.

> Routes of transmission and risk behaviors. People can get infected with HIV from blood-to-blood contact (this includes blood transfusions, sharing needles when using injectable illicit drugs) or sexual contact (including multiple partners, lack of use of safer sex practices).

> Present correct information and dispel misconceptions, such as the misbelief that HIV can be "caught" by touching a person who has HIV. For more specific information on teaching about HIV, you may want to invite a guest speaker from the local Public Health department or other agency who is knowledgeable about STIs. It is important that the speaker has the ability to present the information at the level that the participants will understand and find useful.

SECTION 5: SEXUAL AWARENESS

GOAL 11: Discussing Other Health Issues Related to Sexual Awareness

Activities

1. Review the importance of keeping the whole body clean. As an adult, there is a need for deodorant and possibly more frequent bathing, showering, or washing.

   Hygiene

2. You might also want to discuss the importance of behaviors that promote health, including eating nutritious foods, getting enough sleep, and exercising.

   Health Behaviors

3. Discuss the effect of using drugs (including prescription drugs) and alcohol on judgement about sexual behavior. A person who is under the influence of alcohol or drugs is more likely to lack judgment about engaging in sexual intercourse, to find themselves in dangerous situations such as being exposed to sexually transmitted infections, or to be a victim of sexual assault.

   Drugs and Alcohol

4. If someone shares that they are feeling pressured to use drugs and alcohol, address how this may affect judgment in sexual behavior and where they can find support.

Community or Informal Activities

1. Look for opportunities in daily life to reinforce learning and answer questions related to sexuality. Seize the "teachable moment."

2. It may be necessary to assist individuals in preparing for and participating in physical (including gynecological) exams. You may assist them in finding sensitive health care providers who offer support to the person and who assist in increasing the person's awareness and comfort with sexuality.

SECTION 6
ASSERTIVENESS

- Increasing Self-Empowerment Through Word and Actions

- Recognizing a Situation as Potentially Unsafe

- Learning to Say "No" and Using Basic Self-Protection

- Knowing How and Where to Get Help at Home and in the Community

- Reporting Sexual Harassment or Assault

"Perpetrators pick people who are less powerful than they are. Sexual assault is an abuse of power and relationships between people."
— A sex therapist

Assertiveness is highly valued in our society. Learning to communicate and behave in ways that preserve our dignity and individuality and protect our personal interests is something we all seek and value. When people with developmental disabilities develop skills to express their needs, desires, choices, and opinions, they can then protect themselves from exploitative or abusive relationships, and also develop and sustain healthy relationships. The behaviors involved in meeting new people, asking, and accepting or turning down a social invitation all require assertiveness.

Being assertive is especially difficult for people who have been taught to be dependent, to be passive and compliant, and to trust others' opinions about what is best for them. It is best to foster choice making, encouraging the opportunity to practice and to make real choices in both small and important areas of the person's life.

"Projecting an assertive image discourages abuse. Once protective behaviors have been learned, it becomes part of daily life in work, in social relationships, and in the family."

— A rape crisis worker

While assertiveness training should include "stranger danger" concepts, the focus should clearly be on learning to be assertive with people with whom the participants have ongoing relationships or contact. We know that 90% of sexual abuse of people with developmental disabilities is perpetrated by someone the victim knows. It is crucial to help participants assert themselves with the friends, family, and support providers. Since a growing threat is perpetrators seeking victims on the internet, it is crucial that participants who use the internet learn safety skills. For individuals who are not able to learn assertiveness behaviors and who are highly vulnerable (for example, people who have severe/profound intellectual disabilities), the family and support providers need to develop a safety net for assuring a safe environment.

Research tells us that victims of sexual abuse are frequently chosen not because of their sexual attractiveness, but because of their perceived powerlessness and non-assertive demeanor. People with developmental disabilities are frequently viewed as easy targets by perpetrators. Sex offenders often assume they will not understand what is happening to them and that they will not be able to defend themselves against assault, nor are they able to tell others about the incident. To counter these assumptions, personal empowerment needs to be an essential part of any program aimed at the prevention of abuse.

GOAL 1: Increasing Self-Empowerment Through Words and Actions

Activities:

1. Group sharing. Have participants take turns telling the group about something good that happened to them during the week. Focus on the successes that individuals experienced during the week, problems they solved, or situations they feel they handled well.

2. Group discussion. What are some of the things in your life that you would like to change? What are you happy with and what do you want to keep the same?

3. Group discussion. Talk about how we express our feelings and how we can let others know what we want or need. Have group members practice using words and demonstrating actions that they can use to tell others what they need, want, or don't want.

Expressing Feelings, Wants, and Needs

4. Role-play. Practice situations in which the individual makes a choice and conveys that choice to another person. For example: You are in a store trying on a dress and the salesperson tells you it looks great and urges you to buy it. You don't like the way the dress looks but feel pressured by the salesperson. Practice saying, "No, I don't like the way the dress looks. I'd like to try on a different dress."

GOAL 2: Recognizing a Situation as Potentially Unsafe

Activities

1. Help group members identify dangers in their everyday life. Danger is something that is not safe; it is something that could possibly hurt you. For example:

Dangers

   › Walking alone in a dark alley at night

   › Going in deep water if you don't know how to swim

   › Using the stove to cook some food if you don't how to

2. Talk about feeling safe or unsafe. Discuss times when you knew you were safe. What did that feel like? Talk about times when you felt unsafe, frightened, or embarrassed and what caused those feelings. Have group members complete sentences such as, "When I'm alone at home, I feel... "

Safe and Unsafe

3. Review content on "strangers." (See Goal #2: Identifying Persons in One's Life as...Strangers, Activities #7 through #9, in Section Three: Understanding Relationships, page 25.) Review that a stranger is any person you do not know, and if you don't know their name, then they are a stranger. Some

Strangers

strangers are community helpers and citizens such as doctors, nurses, police officers, store clerks, or security guards. Most strangers are not dangerous. Other strangers may be dangerous strangers or someone who might hurt you. Dangerous strangers might be hard to pick out just by looking at them, so always trust your "gut feelings." (See below, Goal #1: Recognizing A Situation as Potentially Unsafe, Activity #6, page 86, for reviewing the concept of "gut feelings.")

Types of Touches

4. Review with participants the concepts of good, bad, and confusing touches. (refer to Goal #5: Differentiating Between Inappropriate and Appropriate Touching, Activity #2, in Section Five: Sexual Awareness, page 63). Talk about good touches that feel nice—for example, a hug from your good friend when you want one. Bad touches feel bad—for example, a kick in the leg that hurts. A confusing touch is a touch that isn't clearly good or bad, but just not right—for example, when someone you like and who is usually nice to you touches you in a way that doesn't feel right.

Trusting A "Gut" Feeling

5. Review the concept of trusting your own "gut feelings." (See, Goal #2: Identifying Persons in One's Life as...and Strangers, in Section Three: Understanding Relationships, Activity #10, Page 25). Talk about how you feel when you are scared—your heart pounds, you breathe quickly, and your hands sweat. This means your body is responding to something that isn't quite right. Sometimes, you may feel these "scared" feelings when you are around a stranger. You might also feel these "scared" feelings when you're around someone you know. Pay attention to the way you feel inside and the way your body feels outside; be in touch with your feelings.

Sexual Assault

6. Discuss sexual assault. Begin by reviewing sexual body parts, (see Goal #3: Identifying Body Parts and Understanding Their Functions, in Section Five: Sexual Awareness, pages 57) and appropriate and inappropriate touching (see Goal #5: Differentiating Between Inappropriate and Appropriate Touching, in Section Five: Sexual Awareness, pages 62). Anatomically correct dolls can be helpful here. Be careful to end this discussion on a positive note—that there are ways to protect yourself from sexual assault.

➤ Define sexual assault. Sexual assault, also known as sexual abuse, is when someone engages in sexual activity with another person (for example, touching the private parts or having intercourse), without their permission or against their will. This would feel like a "bad" or "confusing" touch. Sexual assault is also when anyone shows their private parts to another person or asks the other person to touch their private parts for sexual excitement without their permission or against their will. The person doing the sexual assault could be a familiar person or a stranger.

➤ Talk about rape. Carefully explain what it means. Rape usually means vaginal or anal intercourse without the person's permission or against their will.

➤ Where can sexual assault happen? It can happen almost anywhere, so it is important to learn how to identify whether you are safe and learn how to protect yourself from the dangers.

➤ Sexual assault can happen to anyone—male or female, old or young.

➤ Who is the perpetrator of sexual assault? Who does it? Sexual assault can happen with a stranger or someone who is familiar to the person. Usually we think of "dangerous" strangers as the people who do the sexual assault... and we certainly must be careful of these people. Very often, though, sexual assault takes place with someone the person knows. You cannot tell if a person is safe or not by how they look.

➤ You need to trust your "gut feelings." There are ways to protect you from sexual assault.

GOAL 3: Learning to Say "No" and to Use Basic Self-Protection

Activities

1. Review with group members the two main ways we express to others what we want, need, and feel: *words* or what we say, and *actions* or what we do.

Saying "No"

2. Group discussion. We have a right to say "no." No one should be touched unless he/she allows it. It is all right to say "no."

3. Role-plays. Help participants practice using words to say "no." Sometimes you say "no" gently; sometimes you say "no" very strongly.

   ➤ Start with situations where participants can practice using the gentle "no," such as when one person has been invited to do something by another that the first doesn't want to do. For example: Your friend asks you to go bike riding. You are tired and don't want to go. Practice saying "no, not today." Combine the role-play with group discussion about how it feels to say "no" to a friend.

   ➤ Continue with situations to practice using the strong "no," where it seems one person is trying to hurt another person or is trying to get the person to do something that the second person doesn't want to do. Responding with a strong "no" is necessary. For example: Two people are out on a date, and one person makes unwanted sexual advances, (which means trying to touch the person intimately or on a private part). Practice saying a strong "no. "

   ➤ Help participants think of other strong statements, such as "leave me alone," "I don't want to," and "stop that." Talk about how this situation would feel, how to handle the situation if the unwanted behavior continues, and whether the group members would ever consider going on another date with the person.

4. Have group members practice saying "no" in various ways using actions including facial expressions and body language. To get the idea, you might first show group members pictures of facial expressions such as "serious," "angry," or "firm," as well as pictures of body postures that express strong actions. Ask the group members if the pictures are saying "yes" or "no." Role-play situations in which participants use facial expressions and body language to indicate "no."

5. "What Would You Do?" Explain to group members that if they use words and actions together, the message will be even stronger. Give the students situations and help them to figure out, "What if that happened...? What would I do or say?" Remember to practice using words and actions. You could do this activity by having individuals demonstrate their responses or having the group respond together. Use role-plays for the statements that are not sexual in nature. Following are some examples of "What would you do?" questions.

SECTION 6: ASSERTIVENESS

What would you do if:

➤ A stranger wants you to go for a walk with him or her?

➤ Your boss wanted to touch your private body parts?

➤ The bus driver says, "Come here next to me until everybody else gets off the bus"?

➤ Someone you know shows you his penis and asks you to touch it?

➤ Your job coach touches you in a way you don't like?

➤ Someone you know says, "I want to touch your penis (or vagina)"?

➤ Someone on the Internet asks you for your home address?

6. Discuss the effect of peer pressure on sexual activity. Reassure participants that what they do with their own bodies is their business and nobody else's business. People with disabilities need to hear that they have the freedom to make their own choices and that they are not abnormal if they want to delay sexual activity until they are ready. Help group members practice refusal skills for occasions when an individual might feel pressure to engage in sexual behavior before being ready: "I like you and want to be friends with you; I'm just not ready to have sex yet."

7. Discussion of home safety. At home there are rules you can follow to help keep you safe. Some group members will be capable of learning the rules and taking the responsibility for themselves, and others will require supervision because they have difficulty grasping the rules. Talk about and then role-play potentially dangerous situations. Give individualized practice depending on the needs of the group members. When doing the role-plays, provide situations that allow the students an opportunity to practice with "persistent" perpetrators. Prompt the participants with appropriate phrases. Remind role-players to use words and actions. Use of real props like a cell phone, door, and doorbell is best.

Home
Safety

Telephone Use

> When answering the telephone, say "Hello." If you give any name, use your first name only.

> Find out who is calling before giving any more information.

> Never say that you are home alone or that others are not there with you. If the person asks if others are there with you, say, "They can't come to the phone right now" or "They are busy" or "Mom is in the shower." Ask if you can take a message or tell them to call back later.

> Never continue to talk with a stranger. Hang up if the person keeps asking more questions. If the phone call is obscene (the person starts using dirty language or saying nasty things), hang up.

> It is possible to block unwanted callers or ask somebody to help with this.

Answering the door

> If you are home alone, never open the door unless you know the person well. Do you recognize the voice? Can you peek out a peephole or window to see them? If you are not positive about who is at the door, DO NOT open the door.

> Never say you are home alone. Just say something such as, "My roommate can't come to the door right now."

> Never give your name or phone number if the person asks for them. Just say, "I don't give out that information."

> Never leave your door unlocked if you are home alone. Lock the door (with a security chain, if you have one) and ground floor windows, too.

8. Discussion of use of social media. Identify participants who use the Internet. Review internet safety tips and address issues such as:

> Protecting identity—never give out personal information, such as your address or phone number. If someone asks for this information, just say, "I don't give out that information."

> Never send pictures of yourself or your friends to someone you don't know.

> Never post private information on message boards, blogs, or networking websites such as Facebook.

GOAL 4: Knowing How and Where to Get Help at Home and in the Community

Activities

1. Have participants list safe people in the community who can provide help when needed. Emphasize that police officers are often not immediately available when help is needed, so other safe people need to be identified such as bus drivers, store clerks, neighbors, or job coaches.

   Community Helpers

2. Review the concept of "safe" strangers. (See above, Activity #9, Goal 2: Identifying Persons in One's Life as Relatives…Strangers, in Section Three: Understanding Relationships.)

3. Group discussion about dealing with emergencies.

   Emergencies

   > Talk about: What is an emergency? Discuss fires, accidents, health problems, or robberies.

   > What to do? Discuss with each group member—and their significant other—what the individual's plan is according to the person's capabilities. Consider whether the person is capable of staying home alone and what their capabilities are if a caregiver or roommate is injured or needs help.

   > Role-play. Practice getting help in various situations, such as using the telephone to call 911 or asking another person to help. For example: Would you call 911 if…?

4. Discuss possible ways of getting help in an uncomfortable or dangerous situation. These situations might include times when someone is trying to

hurt you; when there is a fire; or if you are with another person or caregiver, and the person or caregiver has had an accident or injury and you need to get help. The ways of getting help may include:

> Making a noise or yelling to attract attention.

> Walking or running to where there are other people.

> Using a telephone to call for help.

GOAL 5: Reporting Sexual Harassment or Assault

Activities

Safe People

1. Have each participant make a list of three to five people to go to for help if they feel they are being sexually harassed or have been assaulted. Examples include counselors, social workers, relatives, residential support workers, job coaches, and bosses. When identifying people, think about whether these people would listen to you. Do you think you could go to this person and tell what happened?

> Help individuals think about what they should do if the first person they tell doesn't believe them or won't help them. Brainstorm ideas and who might be potential helpers with the group.

> For each person, make cards that they can carry with them that have the names and phone numbers for these helpers.

2. Discuss how to report sexual harassment or sexual assault. Also, role-play possible situations, such as: Someone you know asks you to touch his or her private parts. Practice saying "no." Practice talking to someone about it. Talk about what to do next if the first person they told did not believe them.

SECTION 6: ASSERTIVENESS

Community or Informal Activities:

1. Make sure that participants carry phone numbers of people who they can call for help.

2. Practice using a phone to call for help.

3. Identify safe people in the community besides police officers who would usually be of assistance (for example, store clerks, bus drivers, security guards).

4. Visit places such as a police station, fire station, or hospital emergency room, and meet the staff in each. This may help the individual become more comfortable should they need assistance.

SECTION 7
ASSESSMENT

- STARS Participant Information Form
- Sexual Attitudes and Knowledge (S.A.K.) Assessment
- Sexual Abuse Risks Assessment (S.A.R.A.)
- Individual Training Plan

Social
Interaction

Understanding
Relationships

S·T·A·R·S

Sexual
Awareness

Assertiveness

S kills
T raining for
A ssertiveness,
R elationship Skills, and
S exual Awareness

STARS Participant Information Form

Date: _____

Source of Referral: _____

Participant's Name: _____

Address: _____

_____

Phone: _____

E-mail: _____

Date of Birth: _____

List primary service provider with contact persons and phone numbers (e.g. residential, educational, vocational providers, or case manager):

_____

Guardianship status: _____

If the participant is not his/her own legal guardian, list the following information:

Guardian's Name: _____

Guardian's Address: _____

_____

Guardian's Phone: _____

Guardian's E-mail: _____

ASSESSMENT

We believe that it is important to assess the participant's knowledge and attitudes about sexuality and abuse prevention as well as to gather information about factors in their lives that may be increasing their risk for sexual abuse. For detailed information about assessment, refer to "Assessing the Needs of the Individual, or Figuring Out What to Teach" in Section Two: The STARS Model.

We have provided two assessment tools in this section, including the Sexual Attitudes and Knowledge (S.A.K.) Assessment and the Sexual Abuse Risk Assessment (S.A.R.A.). If you prefer, gathering the assessment information in a more information is also appropriate. Reviewing the assessment tools may give you helpful suggestions for developing an individualized assessment for each participant.

The Sexual "Attitudes" and Knowledge (S.A.K.) Assessment

This tool can be used to evaluate the individual's attitudes, knowledge, and skills in the four content areas of the STARS model: Understanding Relationships, Social Interaction, Sexual Awareness and Assertiveness.

The participant is asked by the trainer to respond to a series of questions, each accompanied by a picture (line drawing) that is included with the assessment. In developing this assessment tool, we found that adding the pictures as visual stimuli positively affected the participant's ability to respond to the question.

We offer two versions of the S.A.K. assessment tool. The first and original version is the S.A.K. Question/Answer Form A: For Individuals with Ability to Answer Open-Ended Questions. While the original version was useful for most individuals, we discovered people who had more difficulty in responding to open ended questions. As a result, we adapted the questions to yes/no answers and developed the S.A.K. Question/Answer Form B: For Individuals with Yes/No Only. When using this version, the individual must have the ability to indicate a clear yes/no.

The S.A.K. can be used:

> To identify learning needs of individuals to determine the specific goals and strategies for group training programs

➤ As a pre-training/post-training evaluation of a participant and to assess program effectiveness, or

➤ To design a one-to-one training program for an individual.

Using the S.A.K. Assessment Tool

It is best to administer the assessment on a one-to-one basis. Choose the appropriate version of the tool for the individual, either S.A.K. Questions/Answer form A: For Individuals with Ability to Answer Open-Ended Questions or S.A.K. Question/Answer Form B: For Individuals with Yes/No Only.

Using the questions from the appropriate S.A.K Question/Answer Form and the corresponding pictures for each, read each question to the participant. Read the questions as written. Use your own discretion in clarifying or simplifying the content as needed for the individual while preserving the essence of the question. When reading questions, avoid giving cues like facial expressions, gestures, or voice changes to direct the participant's answer. Mark the participant's answer in the proper blank on the Question/Answer Form.

We have found that some participants want to know whether they have answered correctly. The responses of the participants can be reviewed after each question/answer is completed or following completion of the entire tool.

Scoring

1. After the assessment is completed, refer to the Correct Answers for the version of the tool that you have used. Mark the number of points for each correct answer in the blank to the left of each question on the S.A.K. Question/Answer Form. All questions have point values for correct answers except for the attitude questions that are marked with an asterisk (*).

2. Use the Final Score Form, for the version of the tool that you have used. Count the number of answers correct in each STARS content area. For each question, locate the number listed under the content areas. For example, find question #1, which is located under Understanding Relationships on the Final Score Form. Then transfer the score (# of correct points) from the "Question/Answer Sheet" to the proper blank.

3. For attitude questions (for which there is not a right or wrong answer), summarize the person's answers in the space under each category (except for Assertiveness, where there are not any attitude questions) on the Final Score Form.

Interpretation of Scores:

1. Remember that this is just one type of measure of the individual's knowledge, skills, and attitudes. It is best to combine the information obtained from this assessment with other observations and experience with the individual to get a full picture of their abilities.

2. Scores in each STARS content area can be used to assist the trainer in determining the individual's learning needs, strengths, and deficits in each area. For example, a score of 5 correct out of 6 points total in the Understanding Relationships section indicates that the individual probably has at least a beginning understanding of concepts for relationships presented in the assessment tool, whereas a score of 6 correct out of 29 points in the Sexual Awareness section indicates that the individual probably has a knowledge deficit in this area. The summary of attitudes is used to better understand the attitudes of the individual, but not to make judgment.

3. After scoring the assessment, the trainer can review the results to assist in:

   a. identifying concerns or knowledge deficits that may increase risks for sexual abuse or that would interfere with the ability of the individual to develop a positive approach to sexuality or understanding of sexuality; and

   b. identifying strengths and positive aspects in the participant's attitudes, knowledge skills to build on.

This information, along with the results of the Sexual Abuse Risks Assessment (S.A.R.A.), which is also in this Assessment section of the STARS guidebook, will be helpful for developing an Individual Training Plan (see the form at the end of this section).

S.A.K. QUESTION/ANSWER FORM A

For Individuals with the Ability to Answer Open-Ended Questions

Record the participant's answers to each question for the corresponding illustration on the form below, or on a separate piece of paper. After the questionnaire is completed, enter the score for each question in the column to the right of the questions. If you need to, you can go back and check the participant's answers against the Correct Answers at the end of this form (page 102).

Questions marked with an asterisk (*) are intended to assess the person's attitudes and are not scored; there is a place to summarize their answers on the Final Score Form.

QUESTIONS	Possible Points	Points Correct
1. Mary and John are coming home from a date. They like each other very much. Is it okay for them to hug?	*	*
2. Joe is home alone. Someone knocks at the door. What should he do? (1 point)	1	
3. Mary is sitting on the couch with Jane, her cousin. Is it okay for Jane to touch Mary's breast? (1 point) If it is not okay, whom could Mary tell? (1 point) What should Mary do if the first person she tells does not listen? (1 point)	3	
4. Jack is alone in his bedroom with the door closed. He is touching his penis. It feels good. Is this okay? (*) Do you know another word for this activity? (1 point)	* 1	* _____
5. Jean is alone in her bedroom with the door closed. She is touching her clitoris and vulva. It feels good. Is this okay? (*) Do you know another word for this activity? (1 point)	* 1	* _____
6. John is at work. He is rubbing his pants to make his penis feel good. Is this okay? (1 point)	1	
7. John is hitchhiking (getting a ride from a stranger). Is this okay? (1 point)	1	

SECTION 7: ASSESSMENT

QUESTIONS	Possible Points	Points Correct
8. Larry and Sam are gay males and love each other. Is it okay for them to touch each other's penis in private? (*)	*	*
9. Jenny and Marie are lesbians and love each other. Is it okay for them to touch each other's clitoris and vulva in private? (*)	*	*
10. Kate does not want Mike to pull her shirt. What should she do? (1 point)	1	
11. Mary lost her billfold. Her bus money was in it. What could she do? (1 point)	1	
12. Sara is using the computer. Someone she doesn't know sends her an e-mail requesting personal information. What should she do? (1 points)	1	
13. Mary is home alone and the phone rings. She answers the phone. The person on the phone starts saying nasty things to her. What should she do? (1 point)	1	
14. Liz is at work. Her boss, Mr. Smith, wants to kiss her. What could Liz do? (1 point)	1	
15. These two people are boyfriend and girlfriend. They want to have sexual inter-course, but they don't want to have a baby. What should they do? (1 point)	1	
16. This woman just found out she is pregnant, and she has told her husband. Tell me how she got pregnant. (1 point)	1	
17. Scott is the only passenger on the bus. The bus driver stops the bus. He sits by Scott and tells him he is cute. Then the bus driver asks Scott to touch his penis. What should Scott do? (1 point)	1	
18. What is this couple doing? (1 point)	1	*
19. Using the drawing of the nude male and the nude female, ask the participant to identify various body parts on both the typical male and female. Record the responses using the charts below. a. First, point to the body part and ask what the name is (1 point each, 12 points total). b. Second, name the body part and ask the person to point to it on the picture (1 point each, 12 points total).	12 12	*

QUESTION #19 MALE	(a) Correct	(a) Correct	(b) Correct	(b) Correct
Toes				
Neck				
Lips				
Thighs				
Penis				
Testicles				

QUESTION #19 FEMALE	(a) Correct	(a) Correct	(b) Correct	(b) Correct
Chin				
Hips				
Eyebrow				
Pubic Hair				
Vulva				
Breast				

CORRECT ANSWERS for S.A.K. QUESTION/ANSWER FORM A

1. Attitude question (*)
2. Ask who it is before opening the door or don't open it if it is a stranger (1 point)
3. No (1 point) She could tell a trustworthy person, such as a parent or teacher (1 point)
4. Attitude question (*) Masturbation (1 point)
5. Attitude question (*) Masturbation (1 point)
6. No (1 point)
7. No (1 point)
8. Attitude question (*)
9. Attitude question (*)
10. Tell him "stop" or walk away (1 point)
11. She could talk to someone she trusts, such as the bus driver or a store clerk, or use the telephone to call someone like a parent or staff person (1 point)
12. Ignore or delete the e-mail message (1 point)
13. End the call (1 point)
14. Tell him "no," or walk away (1 point)
15. Use birth control, or name a specific type such as condom, birth control pill (1 point)
16. They had intercourse, or more specifically, he put his penis in her vagina and the sperm met the egg (1 point)
17. Say "no," or get off the bus (1 point)
18. Having intercourse, or having sex (1 point)

SECTION 7: ASSESSMENT

FINAL SCORE FORM for S.A.K. QUESTION/ANSWER FORM A

For each question, locate the number listed below and transfer the score (# of correct points) from the "Question/Answer Sheet." For attitude questions, summarize the person's answers on the lines under each category (except for Assertiveness, where there are none.) Note: Some of the questions are scored under more than one of the content areas.

UNDERSTANDING RELATIONSHIPS

QUESTION #	POSSIBLE POINTS	POINTS CORRECT
3	3	
12	1	
14	1	
17	1	
TOTALS	6	

Summary of answers from attitude questions (#1, #8, #9)

_____

_____

_____

_____

_____

SOCIAL INTERACTION

QUESTION #	POSSIBLE POINTS	POINTS CORRECT
6	1	
10	1	
TOTALS	2	

Summary of answers from attitude questions (#1, #8, #9)

_____

_____

_____

SEXUAL AWARENESS

QUESTION #	POSSIBLE POINTS	POINTS CORRECT
3	3	
4	1	
5	1	
15	1	
16	1	
18	1	
19	24	
TOTALS	32	

SECTION 7: ASSESSMENT

Summary of answers from attitude questions (#1, #4, #5, #8 and #9):

_____

_____

_____

_____

_____

_____

ASSERTIVENESS

QUESTION #	POSSIBLE POINTS	POINTS CORRECT
2	1	
3	1	
7	1	
10	1	
11	1	
12	1	
13	1	
14	1	
17	1	
TOTALS	9	

(No attitude questions)

S.A.K. QUESTIONS/ANSWER FORM B

For Individuals with the Ability to Answer Yes/No Questions Only

Record the participant's answers to each question on the form below or on a separate piece of paper. After the questionnaire is completed, enter the score for each question in the column to the right of each question. If you need to, you can go back and check the participant's answers against the correct answers at the end of this form. (page 110). Questions marked with an asterisk (*) are intended to assess the person's attitudes and are not scored, but there is a place to summarize them on the Final Score Form.

QUESTIONS	YES	NO	Possible Points	Points Correct
1. Mary and John are coming home from a date. They like each other very much. Is it okay for them to hug?			*	*
2. Joe is home alone. Someone knocks at the door. What should he do? (1 point)			1	
3. Mary is sitting on the couch with Jane, her cousin. Is it okay for Jane to touch Mary's breast? (1 point)			1	
4. Jack is alone in his bedroom with the door closed. He is touching his penis. It feels good. Is this okay? (*) Is masturbation another name for this activity? (1 point)			* 1	* ____
5. Jean is alone in her bedroom with the door closed. She is touching her clitoris and vulva. It feels good. Is this okay? (*) Is masturbation another name for this activity? (1 point)			* 1	* ____
6. John is at work. He is rubbing his pants to make his penis feel good. Is this okay? (1 point)			1	
7. John is hitchhiking (getting a ride from a stranger). Is this okay? (1 point)			1	
8. Larry and Sam are gay males and love each other. Is it okay for them to touch each other's penis in private? (*)			*	*

SECTION 7: ASSESSMENT

QUESTIONS			Possible Points	Points Correct
9. Jenny and Marie are lesbians and love each other. Is it okay for them to touch each other's clitoris and vulva in private? (*)			*	*
10. Kate does not want Mike to pull her shirt. First should she: (3 points)				
	Tell him to stop		1	
	Kick him		1	
	Swear at him		1	
11. Mary lost her billfold. Her bus money was in it. What could she do? (3 points)				
	Ask for money from a stranger at the bus stop		1	
	Look for a telephone to call home		1	
	Ask a community helper to assist her		1	
12. Sara is using the computer. Someone she doesn't know sends her an e-mail requesting personal information. What should she do? (2 points)				
	Give the person the information		1	
	Ignore or delete the message		1	
13. Mary is home alone and the phone rings. She answers the phone. The person on the phone starts saying nasty things to her. What should she do? (2 points)				
	Hang up		1	
	Talk to the person		1	

QUESTIONS			Possible Points	Points Correct
14. Liz is at work. Her boss, Mr. Smith, wants to kiss her. What could Liz do? (3 points)				
Kiss him			1	
Tell him "no"			1	
Tell someone she trusts about what happened			1	
15. These two people are boyfriend and girlfriend. They want to have sexual intercourse, but they don't want to have a baby. What should they do? (2 points)				
They need to use birth control			1	
Don't worry about a pregnancy, because it won't happen if they have intercourse just one time.			1	
16. This woman just found out she is pregnancy and she has told her husband. How did she get pregnant? (3 points)				
She and her husband had intercourse and did not use birth control			1	
She ate too much watermelon			1	
She and her husband kissed a lot			1	
17. Scott is the only passenger on the bus. The bus driver stops the bus. He sits by Scott and tells him he is cute. Then the bus driver asks Scott to touch his penis. What should Scott do? (3 points)				
Touch the driver's penis			1	
Comb his hair			1	
Get off the bus and tell someone he trusts what happened			1	

SECTION 7: ASSESSMENT

QUESTIONS			Possible Points	Points Correct
18. What is this couple doing? (3 points)				
	Are they wrestling?		1	
	Are they having intercourse?		1	
	Are they exercising?		1	

19. Using the drawing of the nude male and the nude female, ask the participant to identify various body parts on both the male and female. Name the body part and ask the person to point to it on the picture. Record responses using the charts below. (1 point each, 12 points total)

QUESTION #19 MALE	(a) Correct	(a) Correct	(b) Correct	(b) Correct
Toes				
Neck				
Lips				
Thighs				
Penis				
Testicles				

QUESTION #19 FEMALE	(a) Correct	(a) Correct	(b) Correct	(b) Correct
Chin				
Hips				
Eyebrow				
Pubic Hair				
Vulva				
Breast				

CORRECT ANSWERS for S.A.K. QUESTION/ANSWER FORM B

1. Attitude question (*)
2. No (1 point)
3. No (1 point)
4. Attitude question (*)
   Yes (1 point)
5. Attitude question (*)
   Yes (1 point)
6. No (1 point)
7. No (1 point)

8. Attitude question (*)
9. Attitude question (*)
10. Yes (1 point)
    No (1 point)
    No (1 point)
11. No (1 point)
    Yes (1 point)
    Yes (1 point)
12. Yes (1 point)
    No (1 point)

13. Yes (1 point)
    No (1 point)
14. No (1 point)
    Yes (1 point)
    Yes (1 point)
15. Yes (1 point)
    No (1 point)
16. Yes (1 point)
    No (1 point)
    No (1 point)

17. No (1 point)
    No (1 point)
    Yes (1 point)
18. No (1 point)
    Yes (1 point)
    No (1 point)

FINAL SCORE FORM for S.A.K. QUESTION/ANSWER FORM B

For each question, locate the number listed below and transfer the score (# of correct points) from the Question/Answer Sheet. For attitude questions, summarize the person's answers on the lines under each category (except for Assertiveness, where there are none.) Note: Some of the questions are scored under more than one of the content areas.

UNDERSTANDING RELATIONSHIPS

QUESTION #	POSSIBLE POINTS	POINTS CORRECT
3	1	
12	2	
14	3	
17	3	
TOTALS	9	

SECTION 7: ASSESSMENT

Summary of answers from attitude questions (#1, #8, #9)

_____

_____

_____

_____

_____

_____

SOCIAL INTERACTION

QUESTION #	POSSIBLE POINTS	POINTS CORRECT
6	1	
10	3	
TOTALS	4	

Summary of answers from attitude questions (#1, #8, #9)

_____

_____

_____

_____

_____

_____

SEXUAL AWARENESS

QUESTION #	POSSIBLE POINTS	POINTS CORRECT
3	1	
4	1	
5	1	
15	2	
16	3	
18	3	
19	12	
TOTALS	23	

Summary of answers from attitude questions (#1, #4, #5, #8 and #9):

_____

_____

_____

_____

_____

SECTION 7: ASSESSMENT

ASSERTIVENESS

QUESTION #	POSSIBLE POINTS	POINTS CORRECT
2	1	
3	1	
7	1	
10	3	
11	3	
12	2	
13	2	
14	3	
17	3	
TOTALS	17	

(No attitude questions)

S.A.K. Question #1

S.A.K. Question #2

S.A.K. Question #3

S.A.K. Question #4

S.A.K. Question #5

S.A.K. Question #6

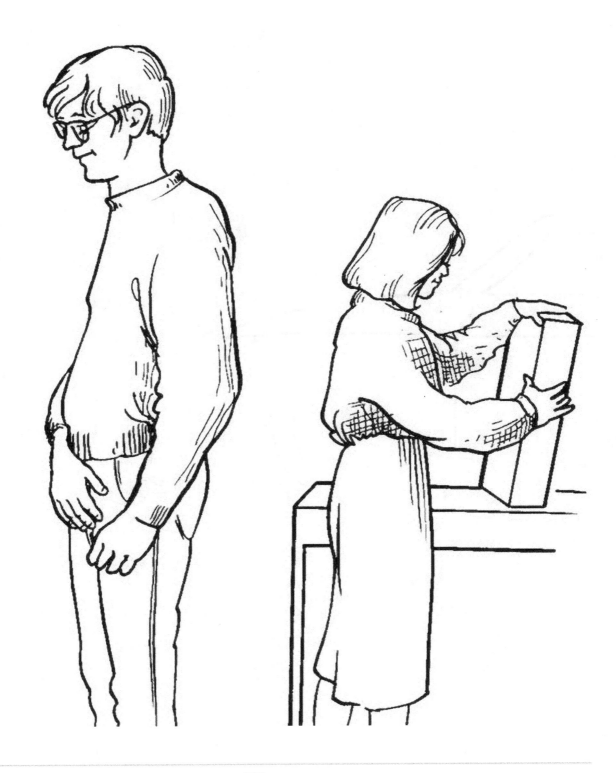

S.A.K. Question #7

S.A.K. Question #8

S.A.K. Question #9

S.A.K. Question #10

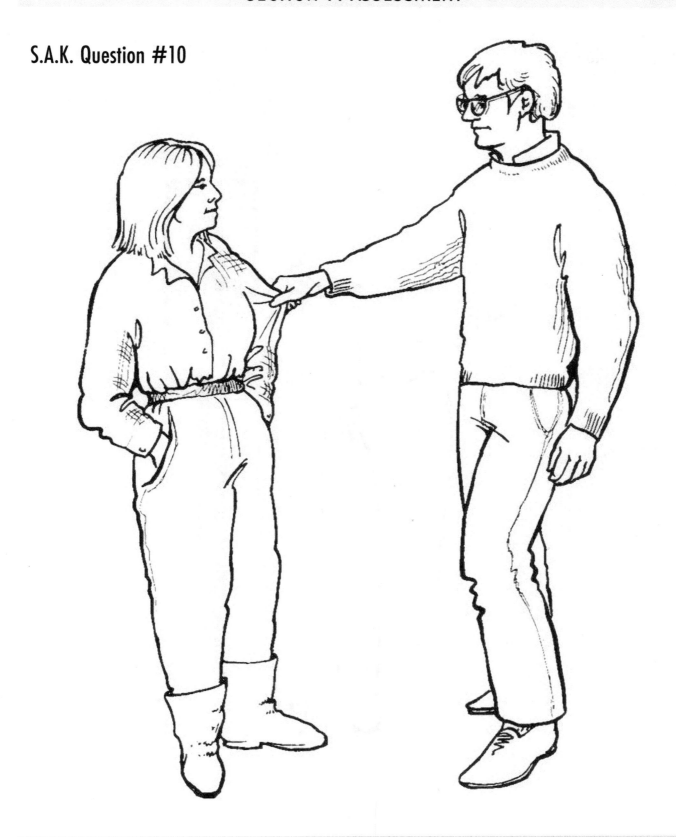

S.A.K. Question #11

S.A.K. Question #12

S.A.K. Question #13

S.A.K. Question #14

S.A.K. Question #15

SECTION 7: ASSESSMENT

S.A.K. Question #16

S.A.K. Question #17

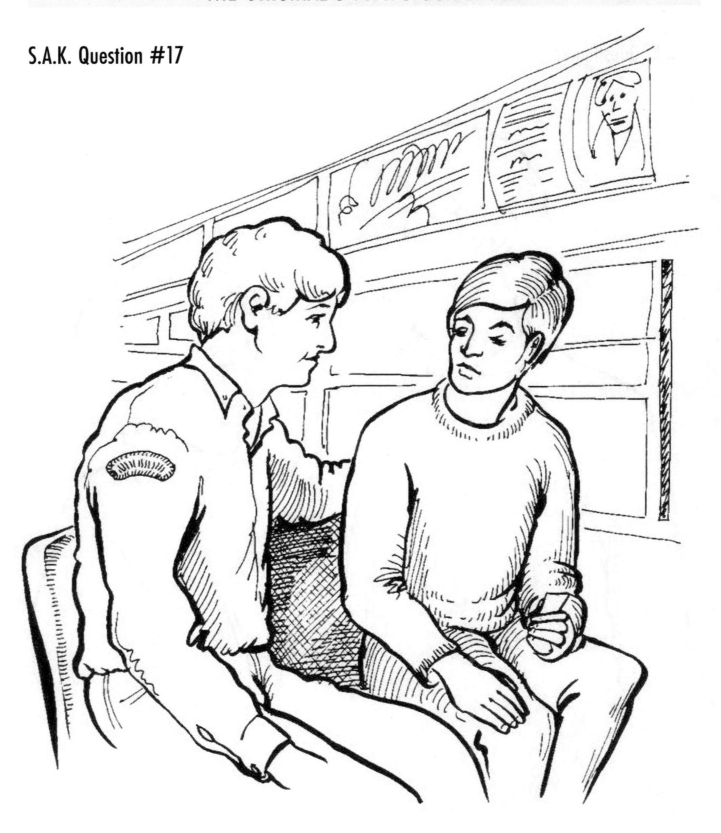

S.A.K. Question #18

S.A.K. Question #19

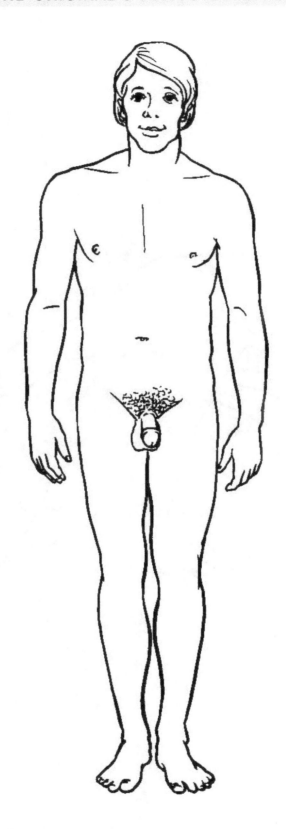

S.A.K. Question #20

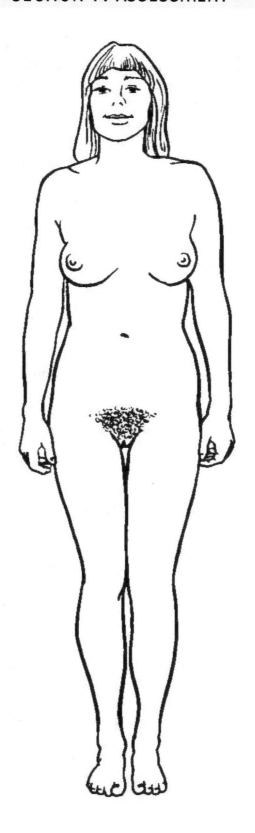

SEXUAL ABUSE RISKS ASSESSMENT (S.A.R.A.)

This tool is used to identify situations or factors in the participant's life that may increase the individual's risks for abuse. It can be used to:

> Identify areas of concern where support, training, or intervention should be focused

> Address environmental issues that may contribute to the person's risk of abuse.

Things to consider for completing the assessment:

1. If the trainer knows the participant well and is familiar with the individual's activities, relationships, and daily routines, then he/she may complete the assessment. If not, then the trainer should identify a person who is most familiar with the participant to be responsible for completing the assessment.

2. To the extent possible, the individual being assessed should be involved in the completion of the assessment.

3. The person completing the assessment may want to consult with significant others who know the person.

4. Some questions may not apply to the individual or may seem difficult to answer. It is acceptable to answer with "don't know" or "not applicable."

5. There is no formal scoring involved. We suggest that you mark answers to questions with an asterisk (*) that raise issues around safety for an individual.

6. After completing the assessment, the trainer needs to carefully review the information in order to:

   ❏ Identify concerns that may increase risks for sexual abuse or that prevent the development of positive sexuality; and

   ❏ Identify strengths and positive aspects in the participant's life settings and relationships.

7. The results of the assessment can be used in developing an Individual Training Plan (see form at the end of this section.).

SECTION 7: ASSESSMENT

I. LIFE SETTINGS ASSESSMENT

In this section, you will assess the physical safety and security of the individual's environments and identify his/her/their settings as places that enhance or inhibit healthy expressions of sexuality. These settings include home, school, work, leisure, and recreation, and other settings specific to the individual.

A. At Home

1. Describe type of residence (for example, foster home, group home, own home, adult family home, birth family, supported apartment, unsupported apartment, assisted living, nursing home, institution).

   _____

   _____

2. Describe location (for example, residential neighborhood, business area, rural, isolated).

   _____

   _____

3. What is the size of the residence and the number of people living there?

   _____

   _____

4. Is the residence in good repair and adequately secured against intruders (for example, adequate locks on doors and windows, and is there a telephone or emergency call system)?

_____

_____

5. Is the residence arranged to respect the person's right to privacy? Are there private spaces?

_____

_____

6. Does the individual have his/her own bedroom?

_____

7. If the person is in a group living situation, does the residential setting have a policy regarding sexual expression?

_____

➤ If so, what is it?

_____

_____

_____

➤ Does the individual understand and agree with the policy?

_____

➤ Do staff understand and agree with the policy?

_____

➤ Do you think these policies enhance or inhibit expression of healthy sexuality?

_____

_____

8. Do you think the characteristics of the residence (for example, location, daily schedule, and policies) support or inhibit the individual in developing friendships (with individuals who are not paid to be in the person's life) and close relationships? Explain.

    _____

    _____

    _____

    _____

9. Has the person or others ever expressed concern about safety in this setting? If yes, what is the nature of the unsafe feeling?

    _____

    _____

    _____

    _____

10. Describe concerns or suggestions for improving safety at home.

    _____

    _____

    _____

    _____

B. At School, Work or Volunteer Setting

Use this to section to describe the person's out-of-home activities, such as participation in an educational program, employment, or volunteer placement. If a person spends time in more than one setting for these activities, complete a form for each setting. The form below can be duplicated as needed.

Work/School Setting # _____

1. Describe the type of setting (for example, public school, adult activity center, community job, sheltered workshop).

   _____

   _____

2. Besides staff, are there people in this setting who do not have disabilities?

   _____

   _____

3. Describe location (for example, downtown, rural area, isolated area, business district).

   _____

   _____

4. What type of transportation does the person use to get to this work setting?

   _____

   _____

5. What are the hours of training, employment, or volunteering?

   _____

   _____

6. Within the site, does the individual have an isolated or private workspace or does he/she work beside others? If isolated, are there other workers in the building or the area?

   _____

   _____

   _____

7. Does the setting have a stated policy regarding sexual expression and/or sexual behavior, and is the person aware of the policy?

_____

_____

_____

8. Does this setting have a stated policy regarding sexual harassment? Is the individual aware of the policy and does he/she/they know how to report incidents?

_____

_____

_____

9. Does the setting foster building of social networks and friendships for the individual?

_____

_____

_____

10. Has the individual ever expressed concern about safety in this setting? If yes, what is the nature of his/her concern?

_____

_____

_____

11. Describe concerns or suggestions for improving safety in this setting.

_____

_____

_____

C. Leisure/Recreation Settings

1. What does the individual typically do for leisure and recreation? List activities.

    _____

    _____

    _____

2. For each of the leisure and recreational activities listed, complete a form. The form can be duplicated, if needed.

SECTION 7: ASSESSMENT

Activity #_____

Describe:

_____

Place:

_____

Who is there?

_____

What transportation does the individual use to get there?

_____

Does this activity provide an opportunity for interaction with persons who have disabilities and who do not have disabilities?

_____

Does this activity provide an opportunity for enhancing friendships and social relationships?

_____

Has the individual or other people expressed any concerns about his/her/their safety in this setting?

_____

Describe concerns or suggestions for improving safety in this setting.

_____

_____

_____

_____

_____

D. Other Settings the Individual Frequents

Complete a form for each additional setting that the person frequents, (for example, the homes of relatives or friends, camp, respite.) The form below can be duplicated as needed.

Setting # _____

Describe the setting, including what the individual does there:

_____

_____

Who is there?

_____

Who is there?

_____

_____

What transportation does the individual use to get there?

_____

Does this activity provide an opportunity for interaction with persons who have disabilities and who do not have disabilities?

_____

Does this activity provide an opportunity for enhancing friendships and social relationships?

_____

Has the individual or other people expressed any concerns about his/her/their safety in this setting?

_____

Describe concerns or suggestions for improving safety in this setting.

_____

_____

_____

_____

_____

SECTION 7: ASSESSMENT

II. RELATIONSHIPS ASSESSMENT

A. *Family*

Does the person have contact with family members?

_____

Describe with whom and how often.

_____

_____

Does the person express positive regard toward family members?

_____

_____

Are there any concerns about these relationships?

_____

_____

B. *Friends (Other than service providers)*

Note: List names and where the person interacts with them.

Does the person have friends?

_____

A close friend?

_____

Any friends who do not have a disability?

_____

_____

How often does he/she/they see these friends?

_____

_____

Does the person want more friends?

_____

Does the person date?

_____

One person?

_____

More than one person?

_____

Is this person in a steady relationship?

_____

Are there any concerns about these relationships?

_____

_____

_____

C. Service Providers

Most likely this person is involved with numerous service providers (for example, residential support providers, job coaches, social workers, health care providers, teachers, case managers, skill trainers).

List names and settings for each service provider.

SECTION 7: ASSESSMENT

Does the person need assistance from staff for basic physical care (for example, dressing, bathing or toileting)?

_____

_____

Does the person have a staff person who she/he/they can trust and confide in (for example, someone the person would tell if something bad had happened)?

_____

_____

Are there any concerns about these relationships?

_____

_____

D. Other Significant Relationships

Describe any other significant relationships not covered above:

_____

_____

_____

Are there any concerns about these relationships?

_____

_____

_____

E. Use of Technology

Does the person have access to a computer, laptop or iPad?

_____

Does this include internet access?

_____

Which internet sites and social media does the person use?

_____

_____

_____

Does this person use technology independently or with a support person?

_____

Has the person received information or training about internet/cyber safety?

_____

_____

SECTION 7: ASSESSMENT

INDIVIDUAL TRAINING PLAN

Name of Participant _____

Instructor:

1. Using information from the Sexual Attitudes and Knowledge Assessment (S.A.K.) complete this section to summarize any attitude, knowledge, or skills that need to be addressed, and suggest a plan.

Attitude, Knowledge, or Skill	Concerns	Plan for Focusing Training/Intervention/ Support	Person Responsible

Strengths:

_____

_____

_____

_____

_____

2. Using information from the Sexual Abuse Risks Assessment (S.A.R.A.), complete this section to summarize any setting or relationships that causes concern and suggest a plan.

Setting or Relationship	Concerns	Plan for Focusing Training/Intervention/Support	Person Responsible

Strengths:

_____

_____

_____

_____

_____

APPENDIX

- Glossary

- Resources

GLOSSARY

AIDS: Acquired Immune Deficiency Syndrome. AIDS is the final stage of HIV (Human Immuno-deficiency Virus) infection. It can take years for a person infected with HIV to reach this stage, and it only happens without medical treatment. Having AIDS means that the virus has weakened the immune system to the point at which the body has a difficult time fighting other infections. When a person has one or more serious infection and a low number of T cells (white blood cells that help the body fight off infections), he or she has AIDS.

ABORTION: A surgical procedure done by a licensed medical doctor to end a pregnancy before the time when the baby would be grown enough to be born, usually sometime within the first one to four months of pregnancy. In addition, a licensed medical doctor can prescribe a dose of certain medications for the purposes of abortion. Abortion is a serious procedure to remove the fetus and placenta done in a medical clinic or hospital. Abortion is legal in the United States, although people have differing views on whether it is ethical or moral, and the availability of abortion varies greatly among states in the U.S.

ALLY: A person who may not share the sexual orientation or gender identity of LGBTQ people, but who supports and honors sexual and gender diversity and challenges homophobic, transphobic, and heterosexist remarks and behaviors.

ANUS: An opening that is the passageway for solid wastes (bowel movements, feces) that are in the intestines to be eliminated. Considered a private part and sometimes used for sexual activity.

ASEXUAL: An adjective or noun describing someone who experiences little to no sexual attraction. The level of sexual attraction experienced varies for each asexual person.

ASSIGNED SEX: The designation given at birth, generally based on a baby's external sex organs.

BIRTH CONTROL: Methods that are used if a heterosexual couple wants to have intercourse but prevent pregnancy. Also called *contraception* or *family planning*. There are several types of methods of birth control including condoms and "The Pill." In addition to family planning, hormonal contraceptives can also be used to treat certain medical conditions in women such as heavy menstrual bleeding or irregular periods.

APPENDIX: GLOSSARY

BISEXUAL: An adjective describing someone who is sexually and/or romantically attracted to more than one gender.

BLADDER: The organ, which is similar to a balloon or bag, inside the body that collects the urine.

BREASTS: Both men and women have breasts; however, a woman's breasts grow larger than a man's breasts during puberty and can produce milk after childbirth. Breasts also are a source of sexual pleasure in most women and some men.

CERVIX: The narrow, lower end of the uterus that has a small opening deep inside the vagina. This small opening, called the cervical opening, lets the menstrual fluid, or period, come out; it also lets a man's sperm cells travel into the uterus and fallopian tubes. During childbirth, the cervical opening can stretch wide enough to let a baby pass through; after childbirth, the cervix shrinks down to its normal size.

CISGENDER: A person whose gender identity matches their assigned sex at birth.

CLITORIS: A small, sensitive organ in the woman that is present solely for pleasure. The clitoris is about the size of a pea located in the soft folds of the skin that meet just above the urethra, at the top of the vulva. It has many nerve endings and is very sensitive. Pleasurable feelings result when the clitoris is touched during lovemaking, sexual intercourse, or masturbation. Stimulating the clitoris is the main way most women reach a climax, or orgasm.

CHANCRE: A very distinctive ulcer that appears in the genital area or around the mouth. It is one of the first signs of syphilis, a sexually transmitted infection.

CHLAMYDIA: A common type of sexually transmitted infection (STI). Males usually have symptoms that cause them to seek treatment. Females often do not have any symptoms and therefore do not seek treatment and can lead to serious complications.

CLIMAX: Also known as an *orgasm*. The height of sexual pleasure. Orgasm occurs after a build-up of sexual tension during lovemaking, sexual intercourse, or masturbation when there is a release, and it is often somewhat sudden, followed by a feeling of pleasure, or relaxation.

CONDOM: A birth control method first developed for men which is purchased in a pharmacy or drugstore in special packages. It is a sheath, or covering, worn over the erect penis during lovemaking or sexual intercourse to catch the semen when the male ejaculates. A condom is also used for "safer sex" to prevent the spread of sexually transmitted diseases. There is also a female condom, which is made to fit inside the vagina and over the labial folds.

CONTRACEPTION: Birth control methods.

DISCHARGE: An unusual white or yellow liquid that drips from a man's penis or comes out of a woman's vagina. It may mean that there is an infection.

DOUCHING: A method to clean the vagina using special equipment (squirt bottle or douche bag) to squirt water or other liquid specially made for douching into the vagina. It is not effective to use for birth control.

EGG CELL: A tiny cell, which is the woman's reproductive cell. It is also called "an ovum" or "ova" (plural) that come out of one of the woman's ovaries each month and travels down the fallopian tube to the uterus. These eggs are very small, not the size of chicken eggs that we cook and eat, but so tiny that they are seen only with a microscope. If a man's sperm joins an egg cell, the egg and sperm together will grow into a baby.

EJACULATION: During intercourse or masturbation, sperm, or semen, squirt from a man's penis when an orgasm occurs (sometimes called, when a man "comes").

ERECTION: This happens to a man's penis when he gets sexually excited. The man's penis gets bigger and harder, and it sticks out from the man's body.

FERTILIZATION: When a man's sperm combines with the egg which is inside the woman's body. The fertilized egg attaches to the uterus wall and then grows into a fetus, or body.

GAY: The adjective used to describe people whose enduring physical, romantic, and/ or emotional attractions are to people of the same sex (e.g., gay man, gay people). Sometimes lesbian (n. or adj.) is the preferred term for women. May be wise to avoid identifying gay people as "homosexuals" because this term may be derogatory and offensive to lesbian and gay people.

GENDER: A set of social, physical, psychological, and emotional traits, often influenced by societal expectations, that classify an individual as feminine, masculine, a blend of feminine and masculine, or something else.

GENDER-AFFIRMING SURGERY: Also known as *Gender Confirmation Surgery (GCS)*, or *Sex Reassignment Surgery (SRS)*, this refers to a variety of gender-affirming procedures undergone by some transgender individuals, such as breast removal or augmentation. Avoid the phrase "sex change operation." Not all transgender people choose to, or can afford to, undergo medical surgeries.

GENDER EXPRESSION: External manifestations of gender, expressed through a person's name, pronouns, clothing, haircut, behavior, voice, and/or body characteristics. Society identifies these cues as masculine and feminine, although what is considered masculine or feminine changes over time and varies by culture.

GENDER IDENTITY: An individual's inner sense of being male, female, or another gender. Gender identity is not necessarily the same as sex assigned at birth. Everyone has a gender identity.

GENITALS: The name for the sex organs or sex parts that are on the outside of a man or woman. In a man, these are the penis, testicles, and scrotum. In females, they include the vulva, vagina, and clitoris.

GENITAL HERPES, GENITAL WARTS: Very common sexually transmitted infections, caused by viruses, that are painful and difficult to treat.

GONORRHEA: A type of sexually transmitted infection that can be treated. It can be a serious problem, especially for women, because often symptoms are not obvious in females and then the woman might not seek treatment.

HETEROSEXUALITY: An adjective used to describe people whose enduring physical, romantic, and/ or emotional attraction is to people of the opposite sex. Also referred to as *straight*.

HIV: Abbreviation for Human Immunodeficiency Virus, which is the virus that cause AIDS. HIV is different from other viruses because it attacks the white blood cells, an important part of the body's immune system. HIV damages the body's ability to fight other diseases, allowing serious infections to develop. HIV can be passed from one person to another, usually through intimate sexual contact or through sharing intravenous drug needles and/or syringes used for injecting drugs into the body.

HPV: Human papillomavirus is the name of a group of viruses that includes more than 100 different strains or types. More than thirty of these viruses are sexually transmitted, and they can infect the genital area of people. Most people who become infected with HPV will not have any symptoms, and the infection will clear on its own. Some of these viruses are called "high-risk" types and may cause abnormal PAP tests; they may also lead to cancer of the cervix, vulva, vagina, anus, or penis. Others are called "low-risk" types, and they may cause mild PAP test abnormalities or genital warts.

LGBTQ: Acronym for lesbian, gay, bisexual, transgender, and queer. Sometimes, when the Q is seen at the end of LGBT, it can also mean questioning. Avoid using the term "gay community," as it does not accurately reflect the diversity of the community, and instead use LGBTQ community, which is preferred.

LESBIAN: A woman whose enduring physical, romantic, and/or emotional attraction is to other women. Some lesbians may prefer to identify as gay (adj.) or as gay women. Avoid identifying lesbians as "homosexuals," a derogatory term.

MASTURBATION: Rubbing or stroking one's own genitals for pleasure. People of all gender identities masturbate. It does not hurt; it feels good and is a healthy sexual behavior. It must be done only in private.

MENSTRUATION: Also known as a *period*. Blood and fluid come out of a woman's uterus through her vagina for a few days each month. It is necessary to wear a pad or tampon during the menstrual period. This begins during puberty.

ORGASM: The peak of sexual excitement for both males and females. See "climax" above.

OVARIES: Two very small sacks inside a woman's body that hold the tiny egg cells. Beginning in puberty, each month one egg leaves one ovary, then it goes down the fallopian tube and into the uterus. The ovaries make the female hormones, estrogen, and progesterone that regulate the menstrual cycle.

PANSEXUAL: An adjective or noun describing someone for whom gender is irrelevant in matters of sexual and/or romantic attraction.

PELVIC EXAMINATION: A physical examination of the woman's internal and external sex organs by a doctor or nurse to make sure she is healthy. It usually includes a vaginal examination using an instrument called a speculum, and a PAP smear (test for cancer cells) is also usually done.

PELVIC INFLAMMATORY DISEASE: A serious type of sexually transmitted infection that occurs in the female sexual organs, including the uterus, fallopian tubes, and ovaries.

APPENDIX: GLOSSARY

PENIS: The man's sexual organ that hangs from the pelvic area. When a man gets sexually excited, the penis can become hard. Semen comes out of the penis when it is hard, and urine comes out of the penis when it is soft. During sexual intercourse between a man and woman, an erect penis is put in the woman's vagina. During masturbation, a man strokes or rubs his penis.

"THE PILL": A highly effective method of birth control for women, if used properly. It is a pill that is swallowed and that works by preventing ovulation (release of an egg).

PUBIC AREA: The place between the thighs in people where the external genital organs are located. It is covered with "pubic hair" that starts to grow at puberty.

PUBERTY: A stage of human development during which both males and females develop sexually into mature adults, including secondary sexual characteristics and internal organs.

PROSTATE GLAND: The part inside a man that makes most of the semen, or the fluid that contains the sperm.

QUEER: An umbrella term to describe individuals who don't identify as straight and/or cisgender. Due to its historical use as a derogatory term, and how it is still used as a slur many communities, it is not embraced or used by all LGBTQ people.

QUESTIONING: An adjective describing someone who is unsure about his or her gender identity, gender expression, or sexual orientation.

RAPE: When a person is forced by another person to have sexual intercourse when he or she does not want to. Anyone who is raped should get help immediately. Contact a police officer and get help from a rape crisis center. Rape is a crime. It is one type of sexual assault.

SCROTUM: The wrinkled sack of skin that hangs behind a man's penis. The scrotum holds the two testicles that make sperm.

SEXUAL ORIENTATION: The scientifically accurate term for an individual's enduring physical, romantic, and/ or emotional attraction to members of the same and/or opposite sex, including lesbian, gay, bisexual, and heterosexual (straight) orientations. Avoid the offensive term "sexual preference," which is used to suggest that being gay, lesbian, or bisexual is a choice. People need not have had specific sexual experiences to know their own sexual orientation; in fact, they need not have had any sexual experience at all.

SEMEN: The thick, white liquid that comes out of a man's penis when he has a climax or orgasm. Sperm is in the semen.

SEX ORGANS: Another name for sexual body parts or genitalia.

SEXUAL ASSAULT: Also called *sexual abuse*. It is any kind of forced or unwanted sexual contact between two persons, including touching sexual parts, sexual intercourse, or anal intercourse. Sexual assault is sexual contact with children by adults, incest, rape, same sex assault, marital rape, and acquaintance or date rape.

SEXUAL HARASSMENT: It is unlawful to harass a person because of that person's sex. Harassment can include "sexual harassment" or unwelcome sexual advances, requests for sexual favors, and other verbal or physical harassment of a sexual nature.

SEXUAL INTERCOURSE: The act of a man putting his penis into a woman's vagina. Pregnancy occurs through sexual intercourse. Usually a sexual activity that occurs between two people who care about each other very much.

SEXUALLY TRANSMITTED INFECTIONS (STIs)—previously called sexually transmitted diseases: A group of infections that people can get through sexual contact. These include many diseases ranging from mild to severe, including gonorrhea, syphilis, genital warts, genital herpes, and HIV/AIDS. Currently there is also a varying availability of successful treatment for these diseases.

SPERM: Tiny reproductive cells made in a man's testicles. If one sperm meets with an egg from a woman's body, a baby will start to grow. Boys start making sperm cells sometime during adolescence.

STERILIZATION: A surgical procedure (closing off the sperm tubes, called vas deferens in the male; and closing off the fallopian tubes or removing the uterus in the female) that causes the male or female to be permanently incapable of conceiving or causing a pregnancy.

TESTICLES OR TESTES: Male reproductive glands located inside the scrotum. These glands make the sperm cells and a male hormone called testosterone. The testicles start making sperm cells sometime during adolescence and continue until old age.

TRANSGENDER: An umbrella term often used to describe a wide range of identities and experiences for individuals whose gender expression and/or gender identity differs from conventional expectations of their assigned sex at birth.

URETHRA: The tube that carries urine from the bladder to the outside of the body. Males urinate from the penis. Females urinate from the opening that is between the vagina and clitoris.

UTERUS: This is a pear-shaped organ located at the end of the vagina inside the woman's abdomen. The lining of the uterus builds up each month in preparation for the egg. If the egg cell isn't fertilized, then the lining is shed about once a month, and this is called menstruation. The uterus stretches to hold the developing fetus when a woman is pregnant and shrinks down after the baby is born. Another name for uterus is *womb*.

VAGINA: This is an elastic passageway in a woman that leads from the uterus to outside the female body. The middle opening of the three openings inside a woman's vulva. Menstrual blood flows out of the uterus through the vagina to the outside of the woman's body. This is where a tampon fits during a period. The vagina also can stretch during childbirth to allow the baby to pass through. During intercourse, the penis is placed in the vagina.

VULVA: The genital organs on the outside of a woman's body, including the mons (pad of fat tissue that covers the pubic bone), the labia majora (or outer lips of skin), the labia minora (or inner lips of skin), the clitoris, the urinary opening, and the vaginal opening.

WET DREAM: Ejaculation during sleep that occurs in adolescent boys and begins in puberty. It is normal and boys cannot do anything to stop themselves from having them, and once they are through puberty, it will probably stop.

RESOURCES

There are many available resources, including curricula, books, videos, and other audiovisual aids to help educate older adolescents and adults about positive sexuality and preventing abuse. Here is a sampling of resources that may be helpful to you in your work.

Programs/Curriculum

Life Facts: Family Life Series

Published by James Stanfield Co.

This curriculum series is a course of study for individuals with special needs or topics relevant to independent living. Six programs include: Sexuality, Sexual Abuse Prevention, Managing Emotions, SmarTrust, Substance Abuse, and Health, Illness and Injury.

Life Horizons: Family Life Program

Published by James Stanfield Co.

This two-part program can be used to address not only the physiological and emotional aspects of sexuality, but the moral, social, and legal aspects.

> ### Life Horizons I
> Includes content on the physiological and emotional aspects of being male and female.

> ### Life Horizons II
> Includes content on the attitudes and behaviors that promote good interpersonal relationships and responsible sexual behavior.

Circles: Intimacy & Relationships

By Marklin P. Champagne and Leslie Walker-Hirsch

Published by James Stanfield Co.

APPENDIX: RESOURCES

This curriculum consists of three programs that are used for teaching social and relationship boundaries, interpersonal skills and relationship-specific social skills. A simple multi-layer circle diagram is used to demonstrate the different relationship levels that individuals encounter in their daily life. Programs include: *Level I and Level II - Social Boundaries and Relationships Building*; and *Stop Abuse.*

All of the materials listed above are available from:

James Stanfield, Co.   Toll-free: 1-800-421-6534
Drawer: WEB   Fax: 805-897-1187
P.O. Box 41058   Website: http://stanfield.com
Santa Monica, CA 93140

PossAbilities Book Package

(2007) By Rebecca Koller with Winifred Kempton.

A curriculum is designed to help students with disabilities understand and embrace their own sexuality by learning how to make and accept responsibility for personal choices. Included are a Teacher's Manual, Student Manual and PowerPoint printouts that provide step-by-step guidance for examining relationships and self-esteem issues. The topics included are self-image, emotions, values and attitudes, relationships, sexuality, health, safety, and positive adult behavior. Available from:

Program Development Associates   Toll-Free: 1-800-876-1710
32 Court St, 21st Floor   Fax: 718-488-8642
Brooklyn, NY 11201   Website: https://www.disabilitytraining.com
                                        E-mail: info@disabilitytraining.com

YAI DVDs and Manuals

YAI has designed materials to help staff who support people with intellectual and developmental disabilities in teaching about social skills and sexuality.

Resources can be ordered online: https://www.yai.org/trainingstore

YAI   New York, NY 10017
220 East 42nd St. 8th Floor   212-273-6100

Materials that are available include:

> ***Digital Download: Creating a Social/Sexual Skills-Building Program***
> Curriculum with seventeen chapters to guide staff through the steps for teaching people with intellectual or developmental disabilities about social skills and sexuality.

> ***The Relationship Series: Three-part DVD series including (1) Sexuality; (2) Friendship; and (3) Boyfriend/Girlfriends***
> The series includes sections with questions and answers about sex and relationships using real-life scenarios, explanations about the differences between relationships and the importance of friendship, and ways to initiate, build, and maintain and boyfriend/girlfriend relationships.

> ***Sexually Speaking***
> A DVD to help the viewer understand what is means to be sexually consenting.

Books

Already Doing It, Intellectual Disability and Sexual Agency, by Michael Gill

(2015) by Michael Gill, published by University of Minnesota Press.

"A powerfully argued call for sexual and reproductive justice, this book represents a vital new contribution to the ongoing debate over who, in the United States, should be allowed to have sex, reproduce, marry, and raise children." Available in hardcover and paperback.

Asperger's … What Does It Mean to Me?

(2000) by Catherine Faherty, published by Future Horizons, Inc.

This is a workbook with activities to explain self-awareness and lessons to youth and adults with high-functioning autism or Asperger's syndrome. Available from Future Horizons, Inc. (www.FHautism.com)

Asperger's Syndrome and Sexuality: From Adolescence through Adulthood

(2005) by Isabelle Henault, published by Jessica Kingsley Publishers.

In this comprehensive and unique guide, the author shares practical information and advice on issues such as puberty, sexual development, gender identify disorders, couple's therapy, guidelines for sexuality education programs, and maintaining social boundaries. This book is useful for parents, teachers, counselors, and individuals with Asperger's syndrome. Available from Jessica Kingsley Publishers. (www.jkp.com).

Gay, Lesbian, Bisexual, and Transgender People with Developmental Disabilities and Mental Retardation: Stories of the Rainbow Support Group

(2003) by John D. Allen

In this book, the group founder, John D. Allen, describes the founding achievements and history of the Rainbow Support Group, a unique group providing support for LGBTQ people with developmental disabilities and intellectual disabilities. Available from Amazon.com.

Growing Up on the Spectrum, A Guide to Life, Love, and Learning for Teens and Young Adults with Autism and Asperger's

(2009) by Lynn Kern Koegel, Claire LaZebnik, published by Penguin Books.

A user-friendly book of strategies for supporting young people on the spectrum in a wide variety of situations and topics related to maturing and developing more intimate relationships. Available in hardcover, paperback, and Kindle.

Navigating the Social World: A Curriculum for Individuals with Asperger's Syndrome, High-Functioning Autism, and Related Disorders

(2001) by Jeanette McAfee, published by Future Horizons, Inc.

In this book, the author provides a definitive program for developing social cognition, with forms, exercises, and guides for students and significant educational guidance and supportive assistance for caregivers and teachers. Available from Future Horizons, Inc. (www.FHautism.com)

The New Social Story™ Book , Revised & Expanded 15ᵗʰ Anniversary Edition: Social Stories

(2015) by Carol Gray, published by Future Horizons, Inc.

This is an anniversary edition of Carol Gray's best-selling book with ready-to-use stories and new sections, including Social Stories for teens and adults with Autism. This book includes strategically written stories with visuals and carefully chosen words that promote social understanding and teach communication skills for a wide variety of situations. Available from Future Horizons, Inc. (www.FHautism.com).

Sex, Sexuality and the Autism Spectrum

(2004) Wendy Lawson, published by Jessica Kingsley Publishers.

Written by an "insider," an openly gay autistic adult, Wendy Lawson draws upon her own experience to examine the implications of being autistic on relationships, sex, and sexuality. After discussing basic sex education and autism, the author goes further to include wider issues such as interpersonal relationships, same-sex attraction, bisexuality, and transgender issues. Available from Jessica Kingsley Publishers, www.jkp.com.

Sexuality and Intellectual Disabilities, A Guide for Professionals

(2015) by Andrew Maxwell Triska, published by Rutledge Press.

Addresses sexuality and gender identity, with case examples from the author's own practice with persons with intellectual disabilities. Discusses trans-friendly language and promotes social justice and inclusion. Available in hardcover, paperback, and Kindle.

Signs for Sexuality: A Resource Manual for Deaf and Hard of Hearing Individuals, Their Families and Professionals

(1991, Second Edition) by Marlin Minken and Laurie Rosen-Pitt, published by Planned Parenthood of Seattle-King County.

This manual contains more than 250 vocabulary terms associated with human sexuality and 600 photos showing signed words and phrases dealing with sexual terms. Contains an appendix that includes descriptions of birth control methods, large female/male anatomy drawing, an introduction to sexuality and education, and definition of terms. This spiral-bound book lies flat, leaving hands free for signing. Available from Amazon.com.

Social Skills Picture Book and CD for High School and Beyond

(2006) by Jed Baker, published by Future Horizons, Inc.

This book appeals to people on the autism spectrum with color photos of students demonstrating various social skills in the correct and sometimes incorrect way. The skills depicted are meant to be read, role-played, corrected if necessary, and practiced in real-life situations. Available from Future Horizons, Inc.

Taking Care of Myself 2: For Teenagers and Young Adults with ASD

(2017) by Mary Wrobel, published by Future Horizons, Inc.

This book is written for teenagers and young adults with Autism Spectrum Disorder (ASD). Written in a similar format as Mary's first book, *Taking Care of Myself 1*, (which was written for individuals five to fourteen years old), this book covers more mature topics that are appropriate for an older population. It is written in a clear, easy-to-understand format with simple how-to lists. It is also helpful for parents, instructors, and therapists who provide support to individuals with ASD, and it can be used in an instructional or home setting. Topics covered include dressing for different events, feeling anxious in social situations, public versus private behaviors, staying healthy, anxiety, depression, and feeling suicidal, social media issues, sexual harassment, finding and keeping friends (including a boyfriend or girlfriend), safe and responsible sex, and deciding to have sex with a partner.

Unwritten Rules for Social Relationships: Decoding Social Mysteries through the Unique Perspectives of Autism

(2006) By Temple Grandin and Sean Barron, published by Future Horizons, Inc.

This enlightening and thought-provoking book is useful to educate those on the autism spectrum and their caregivers about surviving and thriving in the social world. Having been diagnosed with autism themselves, Temple and Sean lead the reader through their mistakes and the ways they found to improve their lives. Available from Future Horizons, Inc. (www.FHautism.com).

Resources for Cyber Safety

Adults with disabilities are using computers and other devices at home, at work, and at places in between. Advances in computer and telecommunication technology allow persons to reach out to new sources of knowledge and cultural experiences but may make them vulnerable to exploitation and harm by some individuals. Below is a list of resources that provide Internet safety information.

Staying Safe Online: Tips for Adults with Intellectual and Developmental Disabilities and Their Loved Ones

(2015) by Ashley Ritchey, M.S.W.

This is a fifty-minute webinar PowerPoint presentation, part of a series by the New Jersey Self Advocates Project, ARC of New Jersey. Vimeo.com/265441660

Yodisabled.proud.org/resources/safety-onlinephp.

A project of the California Foundation for Independent Living Centers, this website provides a multitude of resources for self-advocacy, organizing, and engaging young people with disabilities in their communities. It provides tip sheets on phone and mobile device safety, location sharing and GPS locating, cyberbullying, creating secure passwords, what to post and what not to post, online manners and rules of conduct, and guidelines for video sharing. A project of the California Foundation for Independent Living Centers.

Organizations and Resource Centers

Alliance of Genetic Support Groups

4301 Connecticut Avenue, NW, Suite 404
Washington DC 20008-2304
1-800-336-GENE (1-800-336-4363)

Fax: 202-966-8553
E-mail: info@geneticalliance.org
Website: www.geneticalliance.org

This organization serves as a referral agency that connects people with genetic disorders and their families with appropriate support groups. It does not offer any direct counseling. Referral services are free of change.

APPENDIX: RESOURCES

The Arc of the United States

1825 K Street NW, Suite 1200
Washington, D.C.

Phone: 201-534-3700
Toll-free: 800-433-5255
Website: thearc.org

The Arc is a national organization focused on people with intellectual disabilities, with state and local chapters throughout the United States. The website has helpful information about diagnoses, services, and advocacy.

National Prevention Information Network (NPIN), Centers for Disease Control (CDC)

Website: http://www.cdcnpin.org

This is a United States reference, referral, and distribution service for information on HIV/AIDS, STDs, and tuberculosis. The network produces, collects, catalogs, processes, stocks, and disseminates materials and information on the above topics to organizations and people working in those disease fields in international, national, state, and local settings.

Planned Parenthood Federation of America

Website: www.plannedparenthood.org

This website is the official gateway to the online Planned Parenthood community and a wealth of reproductive health and rights information, including numerous services and resources. Planned Parenthood believes in the fundamental right of individuals throughout the world to manage their own fertility, regardless of income, marital status, race, ethnicity, sexual orientation, age, national origin, or residence. The goal of Planned Parenthood is to ensure that sexuality is understood as an essential, lifelong aspect of being human and that it is celebrated with respect, openness, and maturity.

The Sexuality Information and Education Council of the United States (SIECUS)

Website: www.siecus.org

SIECUS affirms that sexuality is a fundamental part of being human that is worthy of dignity and respect. It provides information and training opportunities for educators, health professionals, parents, and communities across the country to ensure that people of all ages, cultures, and backgrounds receive high-quality, comprehensive education about sexuality.

Community Resources

The following local community or state agencies may be helpful in developing a sexuality training program for people with autism and related neurodevelopmental disorders.

Rape Crisis Centers

State Boards on Developmental Disabilities

State Disability Rights Organizations

Public Health Departments

Family Planning Agencies

The ARC and other Parent Support Groups

AIDS Support Networks

DID YOU LIKE THE BOOK?

Rate it and share your opinion.

amazon.com

BARNES&NOBLE
BOOKSELLERS
www.bn.com

Not what you expected? Tell us!

Most negative reviews occur when the book did not reach expectation. Did the description build any expectations that were not met? Let us know how we can do better.

Please drop us a line at *info@fhautism.com*.

Thank you so much for your support!

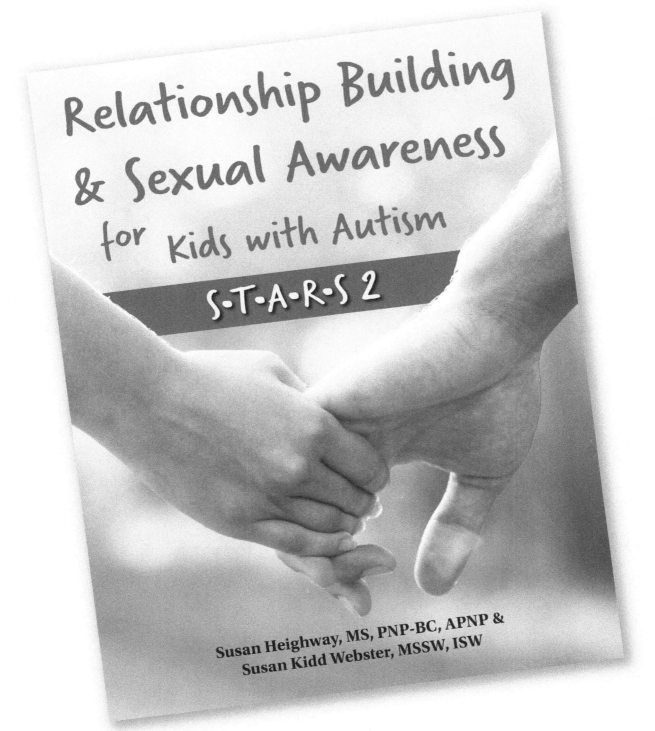

CPSIA information can be obtained
at www.ICGtesting.com
Printed in the USA
JSHW020834170522
25828JS00008B/2

9 781949 177893